Beyond the Mountaintop

Observations on selling, living and achieving

MARK A. THACKER

ISBN: 1499341679
ISBN-13: 978-1499341676

DEDICATION

To my parents, Don and Susie Thacker,
for unwavering love,
a home filled with laughter,
and for instilling in me the belief
that I can accomplish
anything I put my mind to.

CONTENTS

ACKNOWLEDGMENTS

The stories that form the basis for this book were borne out of a trip to Tanzania and a lifetime spent in sales. The central figure in both efforts was my wife, Pam. Needless to say, this book would not have been written without her support. As significant as her involvement was in our trip to Kilimanjaro, it paled in comparison to the time she spent being both Mom and Dad, while I was often travelling on business. The sales knowledge I accumulated over 29 years, came at the expense of my being away from home a great deal. Pam, the only words I know to use to express my gratitude are, "thank you," yet those words seem so inadequate. Thank you also for your editing - not only for catching my mistakes, but for reminding me of the details that brought our trip to Tanzania to life.

I am also grateful to my children – Stefani and Kyle. While being an author, sales leader and entrepreneur are worthy endeavors, when compared to being a father, they are insignificant. The two of you have made my life complete.

Considerable thanks go to Bob Chenoweth, who took my words and brought them to life. There isn't a word in this book that you didn't touch. I was often amazed at how much smarter I sounded after your editing. Thank you not only for your investment in time, but for treating this book as your own.

I also appreciate the assistance of Mike Peck and Michael Kritsch from Outside Source Design for their help in selecting the book title and their wonderful cover design.

As someone who has spent a lifetime in sales, talking has always taken precedence for me over writing. I was challenged beyond my comfort zone by my Emerging Business group, which consists of Nancy Lonsinger, Mitchell Katz, Stacie Porter Bilger, Andrea Brummett, Deseri Garcia, Florence Brown and Dora Lutz, and led masterfully by Sally Tassani. I can truly say that without each of you, this book would not have been written. Thank you for planting the seed for the concept of this book, for holding me accountable to write that first chapter, and for your enthusiastic support during the process.

CHAPTER 1

SO CLOSE

Just past sunrise we scaled the last ridge and there it was: the peak of Mount Kilimanjaro.

After more than five days on the mountain, including nearly eight hours of night climbing on this Summit Day, we could finally *see* our goal – the Roof of Africa. It lay less than an hour away now, within reach at last. But when I looked at Pam as she slowly moved past the sign proclaiming we had reached Stella Point, I knew the truth: as close as we were now to the summit – some 500 vertical feet to go – we still might not make it. My wife was nearing her limit, too.

Pam found a boulder and lowered herself to it. The night climb had been the toughest yet, and she seemed to have little strength left as she sat to catch her breath.

Nearly 19,000 feet above the African plain, the rising sun had begun to take some of the sting away from the bitter cold. But the air remained thin, and I knew the lack of oxygen was taking its toll. Our guides began pacing. Throughout our climb they had been supportive and encouraging, exuding confidence and instilling in us a sense of inevitable achievement. But now Haruni and Ema looked worried.

"Do not sit long, Mama," Ema said. "We have to keep going." I asked for a few moments, even though they had warned us that if we didn't begin again soon it could be quite dangerous. Our guides nodded, but I could see in their body language they were worried. Their jobs were to get us to the top of the mountain, something they had done many times with others. I knew that they would see *our* failure as *their* failure, too.

Pam looked up. She managed a smile. But as I left her to regain her strength and gather her thoughts, I was flooded with my own. I thought back to how it all started, with a wild idea jotted down while sitting at a café in Australia, and to all the training and preparation since then. I remembered scaling the toughest Smoky Mountain trails, pushing our bodies to their limits (or so I had thought). I recalled the hours of hiking through a driving downpour, slipping and sliding on the trails at Turkey Run. I thought back to all the research and planning, to the weeks of assembling essential supplies and equipment. I thought about the five days so far on this mountainside: hiking for miles, at times on seemingly endless winding switchback trails, scaling massive boulders and trudging through quicksand-like scree where we measured progress in inches. I replayed all of it in my head, including how it was *me* that almost didn't make it past the first day.

And now here we were, so close to the top of the tallest mountain in Africa. So close...

I knelt beside Pam. "You ready to go?" I asked, not at all certain whether she would join me in our attempt to reach the summit. Pam cleared her throat before taking my hand in hers. "I didn't come this far to give up now," she said firmly. I smiled and squeezed my wife's hand.

We rose to our feet and lifted our eyes to the summit above us.

So close now. But still so very far to go.

ଔ

Life continually hands us opportunities. To take on challenges. To overcome obstacles. To scale mountains.

Whether your goal is to conquer Kilimanjaro or to succeed in a sales career, challenges abound. But so do rewards. And while it is true that I wasn't alone on my African adventure, it's also true that you aren't alone in your journey to become the best salesperson or best sales manager you can be. Whether you are a seasoned sales veteran or someone who needs to be more proficient in sales, the story — and the sales "lessons" — that follow should give you insights that can help you reach the top of your mountain.

CHAPTER 2

NO REGRETS

I t was October of 2012 when Pam and I began to contemplate a 2013 getaway. Most of our past vacations had been trips involving an ocean and a beautiful sandy beach. They tended to coincide with our kids' Spring Breaks. But now that we were pretty much "Empty Nesters," we began to picture trips better suited to just the two of us. Don't get me wrong; there's nothing bad about spending quality time at a beach. In fact, we have spent so much time plopped in beach chairs, slathering on sunscreen, enjoying various water sports, and sidling up to pool bars, that we think of ourselves as beach vacation experts. (I would even go so far as to say that if beach vacationing were an Olympic event, Pam and I would be gold medal contenders!) But our new way of thinking took root during a "trip of a lifetime" to Australia and New Zealand.

During our "down under" adventure, as Pam and I were enjoying lunch in a small café near Ayers Rock in the Northern Territory of Australia, we discussed how amazing our trip had been thus far. We also considered how great it would be to continue this same type of experience, but in other parts of the world. Just like that, we began to question our previous "vacation strategy." As much as we loved the relaxation of sun, sand and surf, *this* trip had been different. It had been, well, an adventure!

Sitting in that café, we turned over our itinerary and began to individually list places we wanted to go, along with things to do and see. We brainstormed freely. We didn't question whether the destination or activity made sense, whether we had enough money, or even if it was possible. Rather, if it sounded interesting to either of us, it made the list. We included places we had always wanted to visit and activities we had always wanted to do, along with anything that just popped into our heads. Oh, the possibilities! We even did what all good "list makers" should do and added a few items that we had already accomplished – just so we could cross them off. (There is nothing like the feeling of making progress.)

After spending almost an hour creating this list, we made a commitment to one another: we would be intentional and work through it. And even though we did include some sandy beach destinations, we wanted *this* list – *these* adventures – to be more purposeful! We thought about what it would be like to have no regrets. About not missing out on places we wanted to go or things we wanted to do. About never having to say, "I wish we had…"

Moving Forward by Looking Back

Upon reflection, I realized that my aversion to regret has been what has driven me in the past. I have enjoyed a few rounds of golf at some of the nicest golf courses in America when I was in the vicinity, because I didn't want to come home and wish I had played the course. I became a runner while in my early 40's, and after running a half-marathon (13.1 miles), I wondered if I could run a full marathon (26.2 miles). I wasn't sure I could make it, but I didn't want to regret not trying. When it came to family, my wife and I travelled to almost every baseball or soccer game our kids played, because we knew they weren't going to play forever and we didn't want to regret missing "that big game."

So, sitting at that table in the afternoon sun, we became excited about what was possible. About how living our lives without regret might feel many years later when we're sitting in rocking chairs on the front porch, sipping ice tea and looking back. I can imagine that feeling already because I've already embraced the "no regrets" approach to living. For example, I have run five marathons, some with positive results and others marred by injury; but regardless of the result, I know how it feels to be certain that I gave it my all.

Committed to Beating the Ticking Clock

Our list gave us a roadmap for a lifetime of adventure and possibility. But it was more than that; our *purposeful* list was also a commitment to one another. I don't know whether there will be enough time or money to get through everything on the list, but I do know that we will be much more likely to cross off completed items – together – because we wrote them down in the first place.

So several months later when the time came to figure out where we wanted to go in 2013, we pulled out our "bucket list." We had made Italy the number one destination, but we quickly agreed that we could go there well into our 60's and maybe even our 70's. In fact, as long as our health held out, most of the destinations on the list could be experienced well into our "golden years." But we had to face the fact that the clock was ticking. Loudly! I was due to turn 50 in 2013, and Pam would turn 49; and because there were items on our list we weren't sure we could accomplish in 5 years, let alone 10 or 20, we knew our priorities had to change.

Crazy People

We recalled one of our adventures in New Zealand – bungee jumping from a "jump pod" suspended between two canyon walls

440 feet over the Nevis River near Queenstown. Yes, 440 feet! With that experience, the term "adventure" had taken on new meaning. Our friends began to refer to us as those "crazy people." To be honest, we didn't push back against this new label; rather, we embraced it. So, where would a couple of "crazy people" go that might sustain, or even further, this new badge of honor?

We pondered what type of vacation would both excite and challenge us. One that would force us outside our comfort zone. One that might make us question our ability to complete the adventure, and thus, motivate us to make it happen even in the face of a ticking clock.

And there, rising above all possibilities: Mount Kilimanjaro.

Crazy for Kili

My wife had listed the idea of climbing Kilimanjaro; and while I had heard of it, of course, I wasn't even sure where it was located. "Tanzania, Africa," Pam said. I asked her what she knew about climbing Kilimanjaro, and she stated that it was supposed to be a "hike," as opposed to a technical climb. That sounded good to me because I wasn't sure I wanted to learn how to use grappling hooks and navigate over steep crevasses – not at age 50!

Yes, Kilimanjaro sounded crazy and exciting enough, so we began to look into the trip a bit more. I soon learned that it would take about a week to scale the summit and come back down the mountain; and that it was, in fact, supposed to be a hike (albeit a hike up to 19,341 feet!). In my mind, the words "hike" and "19,341 feet" didn't seem to go hand in hand, but I will admit, the thought of standing on top of that mountain did get my adrenaline pumping.

Kilimanjaro made a crazy kind of sense because we enjoy being outdoors and hiking. Of course, our treks up a few trails in the Smoky Mountains were a far cry from climbing to the top of the highest peak in all of Africa. After doing extensive research into climbing Mount Kilimanjaro, however, we realized that, yes, this was possible, but would be very challenging. We knew from early on that we would have to be extremely dedicated in our training. On paper, we could definitely make it to the top; but it was equally possible that we might not make it. This balance between risk and reward seemed to be exactly what we were looking for.

I started to think that if we flew to Africa and climbed Mount Kilimanjaro, we might actually be "crazy people." And that made me smile.

❧

What kind of crazy goals have you set for yourself? Do you do what is expected or do you go above and beyond? Remember this: If your sales goal doesn't challenge you, it doesn't change you. Your sales goals should be challenging enough so you can't be 100% certain you will achieve them. If there is no chance of failure, you aren't stretching yourself enough. Salespeople have long been accused of "sandbagging," a practice where you set a goal for yourself that is easily attainable. Don't let yourself fall into that trap. Top salespeople set ambitious goals because they expect success.

You are 100% responsible for your attitude and motivation. Other people may influence you, but *you* have to decide if their words or actions will inspire and motivate you. Motivation is turning excitement into action. Only you can do that. The great part about self-motivation is you can be motivated and have a positive attitude whenever *you* choose! No one can make you have an unproductive day or have a bad attitude unless you let them. Truly, nobody can motivate you but you! It is for that reason that you should never allow your sales manager to establish your goals without your input. I realize that you may have a sales quota assigned to you, but you should still establish your own goals, fully realizing there will also be company goals to be met. I can't imagine someone else creating a bucket list for me and expecting me to be motivated by that list. Nobody else understands my dreams and ambitions as well as me, so why should anyone else determine my goals, quotas and expectations? You will find that you respond differently when trying to achieve your own goals, rather than simply complying with management's expectations of you.

You must also remind yourself of why your goals are important to you. If you have little interest in the outcomes, or they seem irrelevant given the larger picture, then chances are slim that you will put in the work to make them happen. Taking time to reflect on the "why" behind your sales goals will often reinvigorate you, renew your focus and encourage you to continue. To be self-motivating, make sure the sales goals you set are personal. They have to create emotional feelings that lead to actions. Ask yourself: What will you gain from achieving these goals? How will they make you feel? Removing the possibility of regret from life is a big motivator for me. I don't ever want to look back on my life and feel that I did not live my life to its fullest. Remember, your sales goals are truly "your sales goals," so they need to remain compelling enough, so you will be driven and motivated to do what it takes to accomplish them.

Each time I made the commitment to run another marathon, I told everyone. I knew I could use positive peer pressure as a motivator, and I knew it would be tougher to quit because others would hold me accountable. Why? Because it is much easier to let ourselves down than to let others down. The same is true for sales goals; get other people involved in your goals by making them public. If you tell your sales manager, co-workers, family and friends what you intend to accomplish, then you have made a public commitment. If you really want to be held accountable, tell the world on Facebook or Twitter what you are about to do (as I did about writing this book!). Because it becomes much more difficult to stay engaged once the initial excitement of starting something new has worn off, seek out others to help you in your journey.

While recognition is a form of reward, you also need to reward yourself with something tangible when you reach your sales goal. It doesn't have to be expensive, but it does have to be meaningful. The reward should be something you desire and not something you would ordinarily do or purchase. If you pick something you really want or know you will enjoy, reaching your goals will be all the sweeter.

Consider a reward that will be a constant reminder of a job well done. Provide yourself with visible evidence of your success and it will reinforce the hard work it took to achieve your goal. Pam and I could visualize how nice it would feel to have a framed picture on our wall at home showcasing the certificates you earn for reaching the top of Kilimanjaro; when we closed our eyes, we could even see the frame and the matting that surround those certificates!

Ultimately, there is something very liberating about "taking the bull by the horns" and picturing your life 25 years from now as you sit in a rocking chair, reflect on your past and realize that you have no regrets. Pam and I have lived a very blessed life throughout our marriage, but the prospect of what lies ahead is even more exciting knowing that we have a plan to guide us. We have a goal; and as a friend once told me: "The probability of hitting your goal is much greater if you have one."

CHAPTER 3

WHAT ROUTE WILL YOU TAKE?

It soon became apparent that Pam was as excited as I was about climbing Mount Kilimanjaro. After making this commitment, however, we learned that there were many decisions to be made, chief among them, what route to take.

While the ultimate goal is to reach the top of Mount Kilimanjaro, there are different "paths" you can take to get there. You'll need to determine the time of year you want to go, the route you want to follow, and how long you want the trip to last. I was familiar with making decisions on what time of year to travel and the length of our vacations, but our previous decisions on "route" were limited to whether we should fly American or Delta and choosing between taking a hotel shuttle or taxi from the airport. When it came to Kilimanjaro, however, the possible alternatives for these variables would not only represent different paths; they would also promise a different experience.

Our first decision was to figure out what time of year we wanted to make our climb. Due to Mount Kilimanjaro's proximity to the equator, the region does not experience the extremes of winter and summer weather. It does, however, have dry and wet seasons. Therefore, the best time to climb Kilimanjaro tends to be during the warmest and driest months: January through mid-March or June to October, which are warm and offer clear skies in the mornings and evenings. Knowing this, Pam and I decided to arrive on August 17, so we could climb while the weather was at its best and arrive at the summit within days of a full moon. We had read that "summit night" would be much safer and more beautiful with a full moon. We would have headlamps on to guide us, but the extra light from the moon would be a real advantage.

Choosing the "Whiskey Route"

Determining the dates of our trip was much easier than deciding how long the trip would last and what route we should take to the top. There are six sanctioned routes to the top of Kilimanjaro, ranging from 33 to 45 miles in total hiking length. These routes also range from 5 to 8 days to reach the summit and come back down. The percentage of climbers who have success on each route ranges from nearly 0% to 45%. Not great odds regardless of the route.

Because we had never hiked for more than a partial day, we needed to decide "how big a bite to take." Should we take an easier route that promised less risk, but not as much adventure? Or should we take a tougher route where we would be rewarded with beautiful scenery? Do we choose a shorter trip that is less taxing on our muscles (and our pocketbook), but offers a greater chance of getting altitude sickness? Or do we embark on a longer trip that gives us a better chance of feeling well, but is also more time consuming? We felt like we were going to get one chance in our lifetimes to reach the summit, so we wanted to make the best choice possible. But what should that *best* choice be?

We ended up choosing the Machame (Ma-SHAH-May) Route for many reasons. Although this route has many advantages, being easy is not one of them. The Machame Route is also known as the "Whiskey Route," given its reputation as a tough climb (in contrast to the easier Marangu Route, known as the "Coca Cola Route"). The Machame Route is arguably the most challenging option, as the daily treks are longer and steeper than other routes.

So why did we choose the Machame Route? Although my wife might disagree, I don't normally tend to choose the toughest route in life and it wasn't my goal with this climb either. But there were two main reasons we settled on Machame. First, we learned it would reward our extra efforts with its breathtaking views. We would enjoy late afternoon sunsets at the Shira Plateau, see the mist surround Mount Kibo, hike to the base of Lava Tower, and scale the great Barranco Wall. This all sounded amazing and strongly influenced our decision to choose this route. Second, it appeared that the Machame Route would provide us with a greater chance for our bodies to acclimate to the high elevation.

Through our research, we became aware of the hiking maxim "climb high, sleep low." This means you should do day hikes that gain significant altitude and then descend to a lower altitude to sleep and recuperate. The Machame Route was longer, but it would allow extra "acclimatization days" to help us get used to the higher altitude by climbing high and sleeping low.

The Cure is Failure

The more we learned about altitude sickness the more it worried us. Elevation beyond 18,000 feet is considered to be *extremely high altitude*, and everyone is much more susceptible to falling ill. Age, sex and general health do not seem to make a difference in one's risk for developing altitude sickness. So I was happy to learn that my advancing years wouldn't work against me, but concerned that altitude sickness appeared to be somewhat random in whom it afflicted. Ultimately, the problem with altitude sickness is that the only cure is to go back down the mountain to a lower altitude. The problem with that solution, of course, is that it would keep us from achieving our goal of reaching the summit of Kilimanjaro. In other words, the cure is failure!

So we set out to learn if there was anything we could do to improve our chances of success. There was. First, we learned that the more rapid the ascent to high altitude, the more likely altitude sickness will develop. But we also found out that we could add a day to the Machame Route to boost our chance for success. That was an easy decision to make! We also read that there was a prescription drug called Acetazolamide (Diamox®) that could help you breathe easier and possibly reduce mild symptoms. We also learned, however, that for some people, this drug could cause as many problems as it cured, so there was some risk involved. Ultimately, we decided we would be better off trying to curb the illness before it started. With that in mind, we decided to use Diamox, pay attention to our bodies, and discontinue use if we experienced bad side effects. We also read that staying hydrated and walking slowly ("pole' pole'," as our guides would repeatedly remind us), were keys to minimizing high altitude sickness. So we chose to add a day to our trip, take Diamox, drink plenty of fluids and maintain a turtle-like pace.

Preparing to Succeed

There is no perfect answer for everyone on what time of the year to climb Kilimanjaro, what route to take, or how many days you should take to reach the top. Other variables come into play: your physical ability, budget, available time, the level of challenge, route scenery, and the historical success rate.

But after doing our research we determined the route that seemed best suited to our needs. We believed that with proper training we would arrive in Africa in good enough physical shape to take on the summit via the Machame Route. Yes, it would be a tougher climb, but by taking that route, we would also be less likely to be thwarted by altitude sickness. Obviously, there would be some variables we couldn't control, but we tried to learn as much as we could and be fully prepared to succeed.

We would have one chance to get this right. And we didn't plan to travel over 8,000 miles to Africa only to fall short of our goal.

CR

Before we could expect success in our Kilimanjaro adventure, we had to decide the best route to take based on a variety of factors. Each of those factors might mean the difference between our making the summit or failing to reach our goal. The same is true in sales; the decisions you make, the paths you choose, the routes you take, will make all the difference in how successful you can be.

The Numbers Game

Have you ever heard the phrase, "*Sales is a numbers game?*" While this phrase isn't *wrong*, it isn't the complete answer either. Quantity – the *amount* of selling activity – is important, because there must be enough outreach to generate a reasonable pipeline. But it's also true that if you are not contacting the right people, you will never reach your target. Ask yourself this: Are you merely doing "more of the same" and hoping for better results? Too often we get caught up in some "persistence" thing or just go into "smiling and dialing" mode. It's almost always better to focus on a higher *quality* effort, which involves research, along with multiple forms of contact. Don't limit yourself to just dialing the phone. Consider that the prospect's preferred communication platform may not be yours.

If selling is any type of game it is an "activity game." It is about doing the right activities in the right way and in the right amount. If you focus on the numbers, you just get numbers. Focus instead on the right activities and you'll get *results*.

Should You Focus on New or Existing Accounts?

Did you know that it is typically 5 to 7 times more costly to acquire a new client than to keep an existing client? That's why it is critical to carefully consider how much time you spend acquiring new clients compared to growing revenue through existing clients. On the other hand, relying solely on existing clients will have you totally dependent on the success of those accounts; so, naturally, it also pays to stay committed to acquiring new clients in order to help you avoid the inevitable "financial dry-spells" that often occur. Know this: no matter how strong your relationship is with an existing client, there will come a time when you reach the "saturation point" and no further revenue can be realized.

Ultimately, there is great risk in adopting an approach that relies solely on growing existing customers or only on finding new customers. There needs to be balance between both approaches. The big question is, "What should that balance be?" Unfortunately, no single answer works best for every company, sales team or salesperson; but I believe a good starting point is a 70/30 split between existing/new customers. That balance typically offers the most robust future revenue picture (best reward) with the least risk. It is for that same reward-versus-risk equation that we chose to take the Machame Route. It was a tougher route, but it would give us a greater chance to avoid altitude sickness. We wouldn't have selected the toughest route without a positive trade-off, but we also wouldn't have traded the best chance to avoid altitude sickness if the trip took twice as long. Again, finding the right balance is key.

Should You Focus on Larger or Smaller Accounts?

If you have ever been thrust into a new territory without any existing pipeline, you know the predicament you face regarding focusing on large accounts or small accounts. Should you go for the "home run" or focus on smaller accounts and "hit a lot of singles?" It takes a lot of "singles" to reach your sales quota, even if those accounts are typically easier to close (due to the fact that the opportunity is easier to identify and you are typically dealing with one decision maker versus multiple levels of contact or a committee decision).

So, maybe you should go for the "home run," right? After all, focusing on these larger sales could get you to your sales quota quicker; but they often have long sales cycles that involve more time, money and effort. The reward is greater when you close a sale, but the risk is also greater because the time expended is in lieu of pursuing other opportunities. This approach is *high risk-high return*. If you make that large sale, you can reach your quota quickly, but if the sale gets delayed or derailed during your reporting period, you can also end up woefully shy of your quota. Once again, balance is important.

Winning "The Game"

There is a reason why a baseball lineup is comprised of both types of hitters: those who are more likely to hit singles and those who swing for the fences. In the end, there are many different ways to win "the game." For my wife and me on Kilimanjaro, winning the game meant getting to the summit and back safely. The best "game strategy" for a salesperson and company, on the other hand, is to find the appropriate sales balance that will allow you to build the largest pipeline and the greatest revenue over time. A pipeline can be built with a focus on a large quantity of calls, large revenue accounts and only new clients; but the reverse is also true. Determining the route necessary to win *your* game depends on finding the right balance for your unique situation.

CHAPTER 4

USE THE PROPER TOOLS

C an you imagine a sane man who has been married for 26 years suggesting to his wife they should spend Valentine's Day evening in a Recreation Equipment, Inc. (REI) store? If you're not familiar with REI, it is to outdoor adventure, what Godiva is to chocolate. And can you, in your wildest dreams, imagine the wife accepting that invitation – enthusiastically? What type of couple would do such a thing? Well, my wife and I would be *that couple*.

This Valentine's date night came not long after we decided to investigate what we needed for our trek up Kili. We had been casual hikers in the past and had gotten by on t-shirts, athletic shorts, cotton socks and cross training shoes, but Kilimanjaro would not be a casual hike in the woods; we needed a different strategy. So we read some books and reviewed numerous websites and blogs, and found that most of these sources agreed on what was necessary. We would need a whopping 82 items per person! Unfortunately, we didn't own most of those items. It was becoming abundantly clear that this would not be like any other trip we had ever taken. The mere fact that we each needed five immunizations just to enter Africa told us we were entering uncharted territory.

Time to Get Packing

We are what you might call classic over-packers. Well, okay – *I am*. Pam, on the other hand, is probably the only woman on the planet who takes pride in fitting everything she needs for a week-long trip into one carry-on bag. That said, we would often agree that if we forgot to take something, there's always Walmart. Except, of course, there would probably be no Walmart in the Kilimanjaro Region of Tanzania. And even if there was, Walmart doesn't carry most of the items on our packing list, which included malaria tablets, a buff, gaiters (I had no idea what those were) and water purification tablets. Not your everyday items on the shelf.

Let me back up just a bit: it was a few weeks before Christmas when we first wandered into REI. At the sight of so many Subaru Outbacks in the store parking lot, we knew these people took their outdoor activities very seriously. So it must have been equally obvious to Andrew, the first employee who saw us, that we didn't exactly know what we were doing. Not yet anyway.

But with our lengthy list in hand, we were intent on purchasing the first of many items. We didn't know what to buy first, or what brands were good, or how much any of the items might cost (which ended up being considerably more than we ever imagined). We didn't even know where to begin. So we told Andrew that we were going to climb Mount Kilimanjaro and that we didn't know the first thing about how to go about buying the items on our list. (I'm sure he was laughing inside.) Andrew, like any good salesperson, suggested we start with the big items: backpacks, sleeping bags and hiking boots.

First Up: Backpacks

There's a lot more to choosing a Kilimanjaro-worthy backpack than merely picking the color you like. Over the next two and a half hours we were professionally fit, first by having our torsos measured, followed by deciding on the type of frame, capacity, type of pack, ventilation system, hydration configuration, material, load support, pockets... You get the idea. Not to mention the most important detail: to ensure the proper fit, always load your pack with a comparable weight to what you will carry when hiking. Pam and I looked at one another; at this rate it would take us over 200 hours to purchase the remaining 81 items on our list!

Thanks to Andrew and others at REI, Pam and I purchased our backpacks and some additional items that day. But instead of just storing them for our trip, we wrapped them and gave them to one another for Christmas. Due to the number of items we needed to buy over the next 4 to 6 months, we decided to purchase items from our list for each holiday or special occasion. That brings me to our Valentine's Day date.

The Holiday Connection

Not only was Pam *not* mad at me for suggesting we go to REI that evening, she was excited about the excursion; after all, that night we were going to buy hiking boots! Believe me, buying hiking boots was just as complicated as buying a backpack. But we found the extensive decision-making process brought us even closer to imagining what it would be like to hike to the top of Mt. Kilimanjaro. These decisions would prove invaluable throughout our training, not to mention the actual climb on Kilimanjaro!

Over the next five months we took advantage of every holiday. We couldn't wait to go to REI for Mother's Day and Father's Day, for our birthdays and our wedding anniversary. The more we learned about the items we needed for the trip, the more excited we got. Every item on our list would be vital to our training and future success. Naturally, the proper backpack and sleeping bag were very important, but equally important was choosing the right trekking poles, duffel bags and waterproof gear. All in all, we knew we would need to be selective in what we took with us because the porters were limited to carrying 33 lbs. (15 kg) of our personal belongings.

The Most Important Tool: Learning

So we purchased all the items on our list and began to put many of them to use – along with our newfound knowledge – as we trained throughout the spring and summer. Unfortunately, no books or blogs could adequately prepare us for all we truly needed to know. It wasn't until we got to Kilimanjaro that we really learned how to utilize our tools. It was there that Haruni and Ema helped us apply our learning to the unique environment where what we needed one day often changed the next. Here are some examples:

- We placed our waterproof gear in our backpacks the first two days, but were told by Haruni that it was no longer needed for Days 3 and 4. Why? Because we would be hiking our way through and above the clouds near the end of Day 2; with the clouds below us, we would no longer be susceptible to precipitation. It made perfect sense when I heard the explanation, but as someone who doesn't typically walk above the clouds, it hadn't crossed my mind.
- Gaiters weren't necessary at lower elevations, but were important in higher elevations. Gaiters prevent rocks and debris from getting into your boots and this was especially needed when hiking through the loose rocks of the "alpine desert."
- We knew that our trekking poles would help take some of the pressure off our knees and would reduce fatigue as we climbed. We found them to be very helpful, but learned that they couldn't be used in all terrain. As we climbed the Baranco Wall, for example, there were some dangerous areas with very little room to stand. One such place was called "The Kissing Wall," due to how narrow the path was and the need to get your face close to the wall to maintain your balance. There, your hands needed to

21

be free to hold onto the rocks; walking sticks at "The Kissing Wall" were not only unnecessary – they could even be dangerous.

The combination of having the correct tools and knowing how to use them was essential. On Kilimanjaro, one without the other can cause you to carry a heavier backpack than needed or have your hands occupied while you experience a longer fall than you would like off of the mountain. And while we had all the necessary gear to pass through five climate zones, we needed Haruni and Ema to help us understand what clothing would be necessary from day to day. Thanks to the experience and wisdom of our guides, we were able to make the best of every encounter on Kilimanjaro.

And speaking of making the best of the situation...

Right after our Valentine's Day evening shopping adventure at REI, we had just enough time for a quick bite at the sandwich shop next door. (Who says I don't know how to treat a lady!)

⟣

Every day in life we must use – or lament our lack of – the right tools to accomplish what we need to get done. Shavers, toasters, coffee pots, cars, staplers, computers...these are all tools of the everyday experience. To take on Kilimanjaro, Pam and I had to acquire and learn to use a whole new set of tools in order to have the best chance for success. Likewise, for the sales professional, new skills and new tools are always being introduced. The speed at which these new tools become available is staggering, but with greater tools comes greater responsibility. If you show up for a client meeting or a sales meeting well-informed and in command of the new tools at your disposal, you will rise above the competition. Fail to do that, however, and you will most likely, well, *fail!*

The first step to using these tools to boost your chances for success is to identify, acquire and master the best ones for your sales process. There are too many sales tools to mention them all, but I would like to touch on a few that should be part of any organization.

Information & Wisdom

E. O. Wilson said, "We are drowning in information, while starving for wisdom." With so much information at our fingertips, there is little differentiation in what salespeople have access to; indeed, most salespeople have access to the *same* information. But remember that information can quickly become dated, so it is important to gain immediate access to *key* data. That is why utilizing "trigger alerts" that deliver breaking news about your customers to you immediately could be the difference between success and failure. This is further illustrated by a recent Kellogg study that found the odds of reaching a lead increased 100% if called within 5 minutes vs. 30 minutes – think about that – that's less than the time it would take you to watch one sitcom! This rapid response can be accomplished by using lead nurturing and marketing automation tools that automate the distribution of content, such as trend reports, webinars and articles. These tools notify sales reps immediately when prospects open email or visit their website.

Gaining quick access to the information you need is important, but knowing how to use that information is also critical. The difference between information and wisdom became very apparent on one of our first training hikes in preparation for the Kilimanjaro climb. After many hours of hiking, the weight in our backpacks began to cause our shoulders to ache. We knew we needed to adjust some of the straps to shift the weight from our upper back to our waist, yet we couldn't seem to make the proper adjustment. We had read the instructions on how to adjust our backpacks, but that information wasn't enough. We lacked the wisdom on how to make the proper adjustment.

Communication

There is a delicate balance between utilizing the best technology available to connect with your customer, yet still maintaining the proper personal connection. Many have called a company wanting to talk with a person, yet end up mired in an endless maze of computerized prompts, with no apparent option to talk to a live body. While that can be frustrating, it also shows that *our* desired communication strategy simply might not match the incoming communication channels our customer prefers. Therefore, being flexible with our communication strategy is vitally important.

One approach we can take is to allow prospects to learn about our company and products on their own. We can give them access to customer testimonials and case studies. Offering this type of information allows prospects to learn more about how our company is solving challenges for other – and perhaps similar – organizations. Testimonials, for example, work because they aren't strong sales pitches; they come across in an unbiased voice that helps establish trust.

As often as technology can inhibit personal contact, it can also help you overcome the challenges of geographic separation. Utilizing web conferencing tools lets people instantly conduct demonstrations, give remote presentations and conduct business in a face-to-face manner, without actually being there. In a similar manner, we purchased many of our hiking tools by utilizing different methods. We felt comfortable purchasing waterproof duffel bags, socks, pants and shirts online, but when it came time to purchase our backpacks, hiking boots and trekking poles, we needed to talk to an expert, have the tools demonstrated, and have our questions answered. If REI only gave us one way to purchase what we needed from them, they would only have received part of our business. It needs to be the same in *our* businesses; we need to be flexible.

Sales Meeting Tools

Having effective tools to use when you are in a sales meeting is vital. Sometimes the spoken word just can't get the point across. We all learn differently, so it is always wise to understand and adapt your sales presentation methods to the communication channel preferences of your audience.

For example, you might have endured what many people call "Death by PowerPoint," that state of boredom and fatigue induced by information overload during slideshow presentations. PowerPoint might be the best tool to use in some situations, but a simple sales sheet with a brief outline of your product may be all you need in others.

Keep in mind that the ways in which brands and customers interact are always changing, with traditional (sometimes derided as "old school") methods of advertising and marketing becoming less effective. For example, some people respond best to strong visual messaging and would prefer video. Today, companies can use video to inform, educate and entertain customers in many different contexts. There are also learners that can't be told what to do; these learners need to be more hands-on and often need to see a product in action to fully grasp its value and potential. Demonstrations can often validate a salesperson's claim of quality and performance through illustration. Having multiple tools is important in any sales meeting, but making sure you know which to use is even more important.

Reporting

There is likely no more important tool for a sales team than a CRM (Customer Relationship Management) system. It is the foundational tool in every sales organization, the one through which sales teams must manage every customer interaction. Not only is a CRM important for salespeople, it should be accessible and used by everyone who touches the prospect-to-client process. When used properly, it provides the sales analytics that measure performance and guide future actions. Every organization needs to understand the impact of its sales and marketing programs on their bottom line, yet very few organizations have a clear picture of where they should spend more and where they should spend less. Sales analytics can provide leaders with the intelligence and transparency to optimize their business and drive decision-making at all levels of the organization.

A CRM should also be used as the foundation for sales forecasts. Forecasting not only provides a business with valuable information it can use to make decisions about the future of the organization, it is also a valuable tool for salespeople, because it gives them direction on the size of pipeline needed to achieve their quotas. On Kilimanjaro, Haruni and Ema were our CRM. They provided us with feedback on our performance, insights into what lay ahead, and a roadmap toward our goal. Without their insights, we would have been wandering around the mountain with no idea of how we were doing or where we were going.

Bottom Line

Effort and skill will take you a long way toward attaining your sales quota (or even toward the peak of Kilimanjaro), but without the proper tools, the journey will be much more difficult. And even though we had the proper tools, that still wasn't enough. We needed the guidance of Haruni and Ema to understand how best to *use* those tools.

The beauty of growing older is that we realize that we *don't* know it all. We seek out those that are ahead of us on the journey and we allow ourselves to be guided by their wisdom. That has been true for me in my sales career and it was why we relied so heavily on our guides who had, after all, been up and down Kilimanjaro over 100 times.

CHAPTER 5

WELL-TRAVELLED KITTY LITTER

P am and I found ourselves rapidly descending the Bullhead Trail on Mount LeConte in the Great Smoky Mountains on our 27th wedding anniversary. It was June 21st and we were 8 hours into what turned out to be a 10-hour hike. It was getting dark, and we were getting worried. Truth is, we should have known something was amiss after the first couple of hours, for this hike was much more difficult than we expected. But it wasn't until later that day we found out that the combination of the trails we chose – a 14.4 mile round trip, with an elevation gain of 3,993 feet – were the two toughest rated trails of the 79 in the whole park!

We began our hike up Mount LeConte via the Rainbow Falls Trail. It was, as the name would suggest, very scenic with a babbling stream cascading down the mountainside. This trail takes you up the northeastern slopes of Mount LeConte; and you cross over two footbridges along the way – one at 1.7 miles and the other at 2.4 miles – before reaching the 80-foot waterfall, roughly 2.7 miles from the trailhead. The lower portion of the Rainbow Falls Trail had a moderate difficulty rating. For most of the route we were on a nice wide path and encountered hikers every few minutes. When we arrived at Rainbow Falls we of course stopped to take pictures. After 20 minutes or so, we knew we needed to get going. We had another 4+ miles beyond the falls to the summit of Mount LeConte. We knew we had a long day ahead of us. How long and how tough it would be…well, we really didn't have a clue.

After leaving the other 20 to 30 people who had gathered at the base of the falls, we did not see another living soul for nearly four hours. Apparently, everyone knew it was the wise thing to turn around at Rainbow Falls and return to the trailhead. Everyone except us, that is.

Outrunning the Bear

We had planned to reach the top of Mount LeConte and enjoy the lunches in our backpacks. Unfortunately, it took 7 hours to reach the top, with the trail at times becoming so narrow and overgrown that you often weren't sure you were even *on* the trail. Lunch turned into a mid-afternoon snack that we ate inside of the modest lodge located at the top of Mount LeConte. The beautiful view from the top we had hoped for turned out to be no view at all because of the cool weather, fog, rain and overcast skies. Our leisurely lunch lasted only about 15 minutes. We knew we needed to get down the mountain quickly because the shadows were growing long and we weren't entirely sure if we could make it down before darkness enveloped the mountain. We also weren't particularly encouraged by the people who were staying overnight on the mountaintop. We passed by a group of women sitting outside their cabin, enjoying a late afternoon cocktail, and they asked, "You aren't going to go down the mountain at this late hour, are you?"

In addition to the anxiousness of getting down the mountain before nightfall, we also had to deal with constant rain, thunder, lightning, and two rather large piles of dark greenish-black, steamy (meaning freshly deposited) material – bear droppings! At that point, I wasn't sure if we were going to die of lightning strike or bear attack.

(I have to be honest: the thought of not being faster than the bear, but being faster than my hiking companion did pop into my head. I immediately knew, however, that it would be poor form to outrun your wife on your anniversary!) Our saving grace was that we kept our sense of humor by periodically telling one another "Happy Anniversary!" in a somewhat sarcastic tone.

After barely making it back before total darkness (and remember, our anniversary date of June 21 is the day with the latest sunset of the year), the thought of going out to dinner was more than we could handle. After more than 10 hours of hiking up and down the two toughest trails in the Smoky's, we weren't exactly dressed for a nice dinner. Being the romantic couple that we are, however, we spotted a hole-in-the-wall pizza place on the way back to our cabin. We grabbed a pizza "to go" and devoured it, washed down with a beer or two or... At that point, we weren't very excited about our decision to hike with friends the next day. So let's just say that when our friends asked us to consider a much shorter and easier trail, we replied by saying "Thank God; I mean, sure! That sounds good."

Training for Kili in the "Good Ol' USA"

Our Great Smoky Mountain trip was one of many hiking trips we took during the summer. We knew we couldn't replicate the altitude or all of the conditions of Kilimanjaro, but we did our best. We felt the best way to get ready for the trip was to hike in as close to the same conditions as we would find in Africa. Although the highest point in Indiana is only 1,257 feet, our summer consisted of weekly hikes to the toughest trails we could find close to home. We hiked many of Indiana's beautiful state parks, including Turkey Run, McCormick's Creek, Shades and Eagle Creek. We also hiked the Siltstone Trail in the Jefferson Memorial Forest near Louisville. It was a "rugged" trail that was 13.4 miles roundtrip and took 9 hours to complete. It was almost as difficult as the Great Smoky Mountains trails, but without the fear of being eaten by bears.

I learned while training to run a marathon that you should never try to do something on race day that you have not already attempted in practice. So we set out to use all of our equipment and find the best approach to hiking in long and tough conditions. We needed to understand how hard we could push ourselves and when we needed to take a break. We had to learn how to *listen* to our bodies, not only from an exertion standpoint, but also to realize when we needed to refuel our bodies to keep them from breaking down. We read that getting dehydrated was one of the worst things that could happen to you while climbing Kilimanjaro, so we had to learn how often to drink water. It wasn't only a matter of how often and how much to drink; it was also about getting used to drinking from a camelback water bladder. A camelback water bladder is a hydration system that fits inside your backpack. It contains a reservoir or "bladder" commonly made of rubber. The reservoir contains a capped mouth for filling with liquid and a hose that allows the wearer to drink hands-free. In addition to hydration, we also needed to understand how frequently to eat snacks, and find snacks that not only tasted good, but that our systems tolerated well.

We trained in hot, warm and cool temperatures, which helped us to better understand how to layer our clothing to keep our bodies at optimal temperatures. It was also important to wear clothing we intended to wear hiking up Kilimanjaro to make sure it would be comfortable. We hiked in the rain a few times, which gave us an opportunity to use our backpack covers and to wear clothing that would keep us dry, but not cause us to become overheated. We also needed to get used to all the other equipment we were going to wear – mainly, our hiking boots and backpack. We were told at REI that our hiking boots were the most important piece of equipment we would buy and we needed to make sure that our boots were comfortable and well-worn. We estimated that we had over one hundred miles on our boots before our trip so we were confident that they were properly broken in. We also needed to get used to our backpacks, specifically, how to make proper adjustments to the load to not put too much stress on our bodies. An improper adjustment on your backpack doesn't always present itself right away, so our longer hikes allowed us to learn what adjustments were necessary to be comfortable over the course of a long day. We also had to get used to using our trekking poles, which would eliminate much stress to our knees.

Now, About that Kitty Litter

Our goal was not only to show up in Tanzania with the proper training, but also to make sure we had the right equipment and feel comfortable using it. As crazy as our trip to the top of Mount LeConte was on our anniversary, it did help us appreciate what it would take to hike on consecutive days, something that we had not yet tried. Like our Great Smoky Mountain hikes, each subsequent hike helped us get in shape and feel more comfortable with what would be needed on the biggest hike of our lives.

The items that might have helped us the most were simply two bags of kitty litter. We had read that we needed to simulate the weight in our backpacks that we would carry on Kilimanjaro; so I purchased two 10 lb. bags of kitty litter. The shape and weight of the kitty litter bags fit perfectly into our packs! Those kitty litter bags have been through quite a bit: cold and warm weather, rain, fog, through mud and streams and to a couple of mountaintops. When it was time to take these well-traveled kitty litter bags out of our backpacks before the flight to Tanzania, I didn't have the heart to throw them away. We had been through so much together!

CR

I have never understood why so many salespeople practice in front of their customers. The risk of trying something new in an important sales meeting is extremely high, especially if you only have one chance to make a good impression; yet salespeople often choose to field questions from prospects about value, price, competitive positioning and functionality for the first time *in front of the customer.* I don't know about you, but the first time I try something I am typically not as proficient as I am after practicing. That is why a football team doesn't hone its craft in front of a packed stadium; likewise, salespeople should practice away from the limelight.

Before practicing, determine what you want to accomplish. It might sound simple, but make sure you know what you want to accomplish at the end of the sales meeting. Do you expect to receive the order? Be invited to submit a proposal? Gain a second meeting? Whatever your goal, write it down before the meeting. Outcomes are critical because every choice you make before, and during, the meeting – from what goes on the agenda, to how you arrange seating, to how much time you take, even to what food you have on hand – is decided based on how it delivers those outcomes.

One of the best ways to determine your intended outcome is to set an agenda. Effective meetings have a clear agenda of activities that are designed to deliver its outcomes. Make sure you distribute the agenda in advance so people can prepare. Within that agenda, you will need to assign the roles that are needed to ensure success, and identify who performs those roles. Everyone who attends from your team must understand his or her role and how you want the meeting to unfold – you are the "quarterback" – let everyone know the "play" you intend to run and how they can help you execute properly.

Pam and I experimented on our training hikes to find out who should walk in front and who should follow. I often walk too fast, so we determined that Pam should take the lead to dictate proper pace. In addition to the role of pace-setter, we assigned roles for who would take pictures, who would keep track of our medications, who would make sure our water was purified, and so on. Much like an initial sales call, we were likely to get just one chance to perform well, so proper planning was essential.

Practice, Practice, Practice

It might be more obvious what practice looks like when training for a major hike, but what does it look like for sales? Simply put, you need to rehearse the exact words you will use to open the sales meeting, to ask for the sale, to close the meeting, etc. You don't want to trust these important moments to the words that happen to pop into your head. Brainstorm a list of obstacles you might encounter, particularly if you see them frequently at this stage of the sales process. Next, prepare good responses to those objections; and every time you encounter a new question during a meeting, take time to jot down that question, along with an appropriate response. Then, if you run into that question again you'll know what to say.

Step Into the Role

The best method for practicing in sales is role-playing, a practice that can be as anxiety-inducing as it is effective. Frankly, it is hard to practice what you need to say in front of your co-workers, because they already know what you should and shouldn't say. So, imagine after role-playing with your co-workers how much better you will sound in front of your customer! (Remember, your customer won't know when you don't say something perfectly.) Bottom line: role-play works. You don't learn a skill, particularly one as difficult as selling, by watching the unfolding of a PowerPoint deck accompanied by a live presenter. If you role-play, however, you will likely have an advantage over your competition.

Surprisingly, it's estimated that only 15 to 20% of sales teams actually practice role-playing. If yours is one that does, you've got an instant advantage over most of your competition. Role-playing provides a high level of engagement during learning because it gives the learner ownership and responsibility for their own learning. Not only will it will prepare you to handle a variety of different sales scenarios, it will help you identify sales skill gaps that need to be addressed. Don't worry – role-playing isn't about catching you doing something wrong, it is about helping you be the best you can be.

Perfecting Your Practice

We were told when we were young that practice makes perfect. Legendary NFL football coach Vince Lombardi took it one step further by saying "only perfect practice makes perfect." Nonetheless, it has been my experience that very few salespeople do role-play, conduct meaningful research or implement a strategy *before* they meet with a client. We often practice the sport that we play, rehearse for a speech, study for a test, and have a rehearsal before a wedding; but when it comes to sales, most salespeople do their practicing in front of their clients!

I know that if my wife and I decided to "practice" for the first time while attempting to climb Kilimanjaro it would not have gone well. We would have made all the mistakes we made on our training hikes on the one hike that meant the most. It is for this very reason that salespeople need to hone their craft by role-playing and being prepared for each meeting.

Practice doesn't always make perfect, but it does make *success* a greater possibility. So why wouldn't you put in the time to perfect your practice and increase your chances for success?

CHAPTER 6

LEARN THE LANGUAGE

After 26 hours of travel that took us through New York and Amsterdam, we arrived at the Kilimanjaro International Airport (JRO). The airport is strategically situated between the regions of Kilimanjaro and Arusha in Northern Tanzania. We landed around 7:00 p.m., but because we were only a few degrees south of the equator, it was already dark. The Airbus A330 came to a stop, we gathered our backpacks, headed down one of the plane's staircases, stepped onto the tarmac, and took a deep breath. We were in Africa!

I remember thinking the Kilimanjaro Airport looked rather inadequate to accommodate the ginormous plane we had just exited. Nonetheless, we were safe and sound on Tanzanian ground. We moved through the doors toward customs; I was immediately pleased with Pam's decision to acquire our Tanzanian visas in advance. The visa line was incredibly long, snaking throughout the waiting area; thanks to a little foresight, we were able to bypass the visa line and go straight through customs. So far, so good!

After our passports were stamped and our finger and thumbprints scanned, we headed to the baggage claim area. We were relieved to see that our other bags had all arrived. To be safe, I had packed my hiking boots in my backpack, while Pam wore hers. We also carried other essentials (items we definitely could not lose, replace or have delivered too late) in our backpacks.

Settling In

After a little searching, we spotted our driver in a sea of others eager to take newly arriving passengers to their destinations. He was holding a small sign made from a cardboard box with our names scribbled on it. He was friendly, rather quiet, but did answer our questions and offered tidbits of information on our way to Bristol Cottages, our hotel in Moshi. Because of darkness, unfortunately, we didn't get to see much of the countryside during the 45-minute drive from the airport to Moshi. The hard-packed dirt road was quite bumpy. (We later learned that the jostling we experienced while getting bounced around in the back of a vehicle is known as an "African Massage.")

It was late after we checked in, and because it had been quite some time since our last meal on the plane, we were starving. Luckily, the restaurant at Bristol Cottages was still open. The menu was somewhat limited, but it was written in English and the food sounded good (pizza!). And we knew we would be fine when we discovered that they offered Coke Lite – the African version of Diet Coke.

The following morning was a Sunday. We woke to the sound of church music echoing from the nearby Lutheran Church. It was a surreal moment. When I opened my eyes, I saw light streaming through the windows, and I smiled as I came to and remembered where I was. My first clue that I wasn't waking in Indiana came when I looked up and saw the mosquito net we had slept under. But what really made me smile was the music. I was listening to one of the same hymns we sing in our church, but hearing it 8,100 miles from home! I began to sing along, which caused Pam to wake up. I could tell that she was beginning to process what I had first thought – it was Sunday and we were missing our church service at home. But were we? As we listened intently to the music from this African service, we heard songs we didn't know, but there were many that we did recognize. For two people whose faith is so important to them, it was amazing to start our first full day this way on the other side of the world!

Joseph

Our itinerary included a full day in Moshi before we would be allowed to start our hike. This requirement was in place to ensure that each hiker has a chance to get used to the higher elevation before starting their trek up Kilimanjaro. We decided we wanted to make the most out of our free day, so we got dressed and after breakfast started walking toward downtown Moshi. Moshi is a municipality in the Kilimanjaro Region situated on the lower slopes of Mount Kilimanjaro. With a population of 185,000, it is home to the Chagga and Maasai tribes. It is known mainly for its prized Arabica coffee beans and the mountain itself. The city is the starting point for climbers from all over the world and Kili, as the mountain is fondly called, is the gem of the city.

The surrounding foothills offer lush, tropical forests which are much cooler than the city of Moshi itself. Although Moshi is heavily populated, its downtown area is relatively small. We toured the local farmer's street market and visited a number of shops. Before we even entered downtown, however, we were engaged by a young man named Joseph. He started walking alongside us, and after exchanging names, began to tell us about his city. We assumed that money would be asked for at some point for this guided tour, but we felt comfortable with him as we learned about the city, the people of Moshi and their culture.

Joseph took us through the areas that tourists might visit and showed us places only the locals knew about. He showed us the tourist market with higher prices and he showed us the markets with the lower prices that locals would frequent. We began to learn about their culture, as well as some of their language. Joseph advised that we could take pictures of a group of people from a distance, but not of an individual without their permission. Many Tanzanians believe that if you take their picture you might sell it for money. It was helpful to understand their culture so we could pay them the proper respect. We also learned some new Swahili words like *jambo* (hello), *asante* (thank you) and *asante sana* (thank you very much). We would later learn many more Swahili words from our guides as we spent the week getting to know them and their culture.

Pam and I have been fortunate to visit many different countries. Some of our vacations have been to English speaking countries and some have not. Most of our trips to non-English speaking countries were either on a cruise where we spent a day on an island or a weeklong trip where we were stayed at a resort. In both situations, we traveled to places that relied heavily on tourism, so most of the people we came in contact with spoke English. I have heard it said a few times that Americans expect the people they meet to speak English, even if the American is in another country. Perhaps this is an unwitting arrogance on our part that fosters the "Ugly American" label. There is simply something wrong about visiting someone else's country and forcing them to speak your language 100% of the time. I don't know that I have actually had the expectation that someone should speak English when I visited their country, but I was typically ill-equipped to speak their language while visiting. I found that I was, indeed, relying on others to adapt to *my* language.

Although Pam and I didn't immerse ourselves in learning Swahili before our trip, we did try to learn some key terms beforehand. We felt that if we were going to travel to Africa, we should at least attempt to learn what we could of their native language while we were there. Whether it was Joseph or any of the many other Tanzanians we met on our trip, everyone seemed pleased that we took so much interest in getting to know them, as well as wanting to learn more about their country. After giving it some thought, it made a lot of sense – doesn't everyone feel good when someone wants to know more about them, their family, their job or about something they're interested in? This trip felt different than most of the trips we had taken in the past. It wasn't the fact that we could say "*jambo*" to a Tanzanian that we met; it was more about becoming integrated into their culture. It was less about taking and more about giving. It was about making a connection. From the moment Pam and I walked away from Bristol Cottages and walked toward downtown Moshi, it was readily apparent that we were the ones that looked different. We didn't look, act or sound like we were from Tanzania, but we found that when we made the effort to connect with the people of Tanzania, we may have looked like outsiders, but we didn't feel that way, nor were we treated that way. Our walk with Joseph that Sunday morning in Moshi proved to be a great starting point for the rest of our trip.

How did our tour with Joseph end? We spent 90 minutes together, thoroughly enjoyed his company and we learned a great deal. Joseph didn't ask for money, instead he showed us the paintings he and his brother had created. We selected one of his canvas paintings that depicted two giraffes in front of Mount Kilimanjaro - the very mountain that we were going to begin to climb that next day. The painting was beautiful, but the reason we were happy to purchase a painting from Joseph was because we were buying something from our new friend – a friend who had given us our first insight into the happy, generous and humble spirit of the Tanzanian people.

CR

Have you ever caught yourself talking louder to someone who doesn't speak English? For some reason, we have the notion that speaking louder will somehow magically make them learn our language. Our minds somehow believe we are not understood because we are not heard. It is more of an instinctive reaction than anything deliberate. Because we weren't speaking the native language, it was easier for Pam and me to keep that in mind while in Africa. Our surroundings often reminded us that we needed to adapt to *their* language and culture.

But it can be harder in business. When you choose a role in sales, you often carry your own language – words and phrasing unique to your industry, company or role – into a conversation with a prospect or customer. We assume they understand all the words we use and we typically don't even know when we *aren't* understood. While some people are direct and will tell you if they do not understand something, others may feel that asking questions will make them appear foolish. As a result, their nodding seems to indicate that they understand what you mean or even agree with what you are saying; in fact, they are not really listening and simply want you to finish talking.

I have travelled with countless salespeople over the last 20 years, and I always debrief with the salesperson after the meeting to share our thoughts on how the meeting went. It is interesting how many times a salesperson leaves a meeting thinking it went perfectly, but the prospect walks away thinking that if they ever did business with the salesperson, they would constantly struggle to understand what they are talking about. The result is they don't get invited back. That's why the ability to communicate with a wide range of people is a skill worth developing – not just for sales, but for any aspect of business, leadership or life in general. Just because the words leave your mouth doesn't mean the other person will understand them.

Their Words, Not Your Jargon

The key to communicating well is to use your prospect's or client's vocabulary. No one will argue with their own words, so listen carefully to what your prospect is saying. Blend their exact words into your own sentences and statements. It is possible that everyone I met in Tanzania might have understood what I meant when I said "thank you very much," but how unfortunate would it have been if someone had done a favor for me and I responded by saying "thank you very much" and they didn't understand English? They might have thought I was rude and ungrateful, when it was much to the contrary. I could be assured that they would understand me if I responded by saying "Asante sana." Likewise, if you make an effort to speak the language of your prospects and customers, your connection to them will be strengthened and trust will quickly build. If you want someone to understand you, it is *your* responsibility to communicate in a way that *they* understand, rather than expecting them to make the effort to understand you.

One of the biggest pitfalls in sales communication is using jargon. The two most common forms of this are technical jargon and company jargon. Using technical jargon often occurs when technical products are being sold. While there is clearly a need for technical conversations in some situations, we need to find a way to have that discussion without lapsing into the use of technical jargon. All companies use their own "speak" and it often finds its way into every employee's vocabulary. While there are many benefits to having a shared language, one of them isn't sharing that common language with customers. They don't know your language, and frankly, they don't care to learn it. The idea of gaining a sale is to make it *easy* for the other person to say "Yes!" Using language they can't understand directly violates that objective.

Better Communication, Better Performance

Simply put, more effective communication increases performance. What's more, when you increase the flexibility of your communication strategy you will also increase the number of people with whom you can work. Thus, your targeted list of accounts will increase in tandem with the size of your sales pipeline. Not only will your prospects increase, your customer conversions will improve too, due to having a better understanding of your prospect's intent. Too many salespeople make the mistake of assuming they already know what their customers are looking for and then deliver untested messaging. It's a big mistake to base your messaging on *your* mindset, rather than the customer's mindset. When Pam and I needed an answer from our guides (knowing that the answer would help us to be better prepared for the challenge ahead), it wasn't really important that our words were *heard*; rather, it was important that they were *understood*. Being understood meant we would receive the answer we needed – and that would enhance our performance.

Don't make the mistake of choosing your native language to communicate with others. Not everyone understands your words, phrases and terminology; so much can be lost in translation. Yes, it's possible to make a sale and gain a customer by using your language and not becoming integrated into their culture, but it sure is a lot harder. So don't waste your time being viewed by your prospect or customer as a clueless outsider – like someone wandering the streets of Moshi alone, looking, feeling and being viewed as different from everyone else. Instead, learn their language and culture. In the end, you will become one of them, an insider with the inside track to a successful sales relationship.

CHAPTER 7

MAKE AN EMOTIONAL CONNECTION

After spending Sunday morning exploring Moshi, we returned to Bristol Cottages. We had a quick lunch as we awaited the arrival of Gloria Moshi, the owner of Kindoroko Tours, the outfitter we had selected to take us up Kilimanjaro.

While doing some research prior to our trip, Pam discovered that Bristol Cottages was a designated drop-off location for an organization called Pack for a Purpose. Pack for a Purpose encourages travelers to use the available space in their luggage allotment to provide supplies for children in need around the world. In Tanzania, Pack for a Purpose supports the Kilimanjaro Kids Care Orphanage, which serves 22 children between the ages of 11 and 20. A few weeks before we left on our trip, Pam printed off the supply list for the orphanage. In addition to the bags we needed to take for our supplies, we could take two additional bags with a maximum capacity of 52.5 lbs. per bag. Following a couple of announcements in front of our home church congregation (New Hope Presbyterian Church in Fishers, Indiana), the supplies began to roll in -- soccer balls, shoes, medicines, vitamins, sheets, towels, etc. After just two weeks, we had all the supplies that our extra luggage could hold! In fact, the night before we left we were shifting supplies from bag to bag to stay under the maximum weight per bag. We even had to squeeze some items into our backpacks and carry-on bags.

The Orphanage

Once we became aware of the Pack for a Purpose organization and the Kilimanjaro Kids Care Orphanage, we really wanted to hand deliver the supplies rather than simply drop them off at Bristol Cottages. Gloria graciously coordinated our delivery at the orphanage; plus she volunteered to drive us to the orphanage – a 45-minute trip. Gloria arrived as scheduled and we set out along yet another bumpy road. As we drove, we learned about Gloria, her life, her business and her connection to the orphanage. As we pulled into the dirt driveway of the orphanage, I only had time to put one foot outside of the vehicle when I was immediately hugged by one of the caretakers of the facility, Macrina. While Macrina did not speak much English, there was no denying how happy she was to see us. With a huge smile she motioned for us to come inside.

A couple of the boys came out to carry the two bags, and when I mentioned how heavy they were and perhaps I should carry them, Macrina nodded towards the boys, letting me know that she thought they could handle it. We walked inside and saw the faces of 15 beautiful children, along with an additional caretaker. The children hurried to arrange white plastic chairs around the perimeter of the room, in addition to placing a couple of tables in the corner for the bags. We began to take the supplies we brought out of our luggage to get them organized. We stacked numerous pairs of shoes in a pile, set out approximately 30 bottles of ibuprofen and Tylenol, stacked the school supplies and generally just got everything sorted out. I quickly went to work on what I thought the children might enjoy the most - five brand-new soccer balls! I brought a hand pump with me and began to pump up the soccer balls one at a time. After I finished inflating each ball, I would turn around and see their eager faces, tossing the new ball to one of them. Meanwhile, Pam was discussing with Gloria the differences in the over-the-counter medicines we brought. We quickly realized what a blessing it was to have Gloria with us – as we needed to communicate with the two caregivers what each medicine was used for, how much should be taken at one time and at what age the dosage should change – all this while speaking two totally different languages! Pam shared the information with Gloria and Gloria then wrote the information on the bottles in Swahili. Ibuprofen was not a familiar medicine to the women, so it was very important that they understood what it was to be used for, along with the appropriate dosage information.

"Hugging People"

Once all the supplies were laid out on the tables, we began to hand out what we brought. Our practice consisted of counting the number of each item, then doling out a fair share to all the children. The children were extremely well-mannered. As an example, after passing out all the pencils, each child stood up and walked over to us to shake our hands and say thank you. We found out the children went to school where English was taught and they spoke the language very well. Once the first child came over to shake our hands, we explained that we are "hugging people" and we held out our arms to give each of them a big hug. Most of the hugs were the kind that we might give a friend – a quick squeeze and then a release – but a few of the hugs we received were the type where the children didn't want to let go. On one occasion, a little boy named Peter was hugging Pam for a long time. I noticed this and looked over at Pam and we both had tears in our eyes. Peter turned out to be a boy that we would never forget!

We spent the next half hour passing out all the supplies and thoroughly enjoying seeing the joyful reactions from the children and enjoying the personal connections we were able to make with them.

After we finished, Gloria asked us to share our thoughts with the group. There was a map of the world painted on a wall and I pointed to where Indianapolis was and told them that is where we live. I told them about how an entire church, filled with people they have never met, already loves them. After we took a group picture, Gloria told us that the children wanted to know if we wanted to play "football" with them in the back. We knew that "football" meant soccer and we hoped that our lack of ability wouldn't get in the way of having a good time. We went through the back of the concrete structure and saw the playground, which consisted of dirt and concrete, surrounded by large walls. We saw their old and worn soccer balls sitting idle in the dirt, and it was apparent that they couldn't keep enough air in them. It wasn't difficult to realize why the children were so excited to receive new soccer balls. I played soccer for a while and then I noticed a basketball backboard nailed to a nearby tree. As someone who grew up in Indiana, I thought basketball might be more my speed. I shot baskets with a few of the boys, while Pam tossed a soccer ball back and forth with Peter. After each boy took two shots, they would go out of the way to pass me the ball and make sure that I had my turn (another example of how well-mannered the children were). Meanwhile, Pam continued to throw a soccer ball back and forth with Peter for about an hour.

An Emotional Farewell

We knew that tomorrow was the start of our journey up Kilimanjaro and we were supposed to be resting, yet we didn't want the time we spent with the children to end. We finally mentioned to Gloria that we should probably be going soon, so she told the children, and they soon gathered around us to sing us a few songs. We clapped our hands to the songs, attempting to dance along as they sang. After they were done singing, one young boy was selected to speak, and he thanked us on behalf of the group. His English was very good and he was extremely eloquent for his years. We had tears streaming down our faces as he spoke. Each of the children hugged us before we left and many followed along as we walked to Gloria's car. Needless to say, we were once again fighting back tears while we waved to the kids as the car pulled away.

What touched our hearts even more was hearing Gloria talk about how much our trip would mean to these children. She told us that many, many people donate supplies every year at Bristol Cottages, but virtually no one ever takes the time to actually go visit the orphanage. She told us that they would remember the gifts we gave them for a while, but they would remember the time we spent with them for years. We drove in silence for a while, as we were trying to get our minds around what we had just experienced. Spending time with the children felt so much different than just sending money or dropping off supplies. This was a whole different experience – we had made a connection. Over a dozen connections, actually. If there had been a way for us to bring all those children back with us to find them good homes in the United States, we would have done it in a heartbeat. The kids were beautiful, they were joyful, they were giving, and they were humble; and yet, most came from family situations that we could not begin to comprehend.

Peter

After we returned home, we did some further research online and learned the story of young Peter. Both his parents had died and they were buried in his grandparent's front yard. The orphanage became aware of Peter after they found him sleeping in a banana field. Peter had run away from home at age 10 because his grandmother had beaten him so badly. It was hard to imagine that our Peter with the bright shining smile had lived such a difficult life. We also discovered the good news that Peter was well cared for at the orphanage and he and the other children were receiving a wonderful education through the efforts of an organization called Make a Difference Now. What we remember the most was that from the moment we saw Peter, he

47

had the biggest smile on his face. We remember the hugs he gave us and the way he clasped his hands tightly together behind our backs and wouldn't let go. We remember how content he was to toss a soccer ball back and forth with Pam for an hour, and then after they were done, how he just stood by her side. It's hard to imagine how a child who went through such pain could be so loving.

After arriving back at Bristol Cottages, we thanked Gloria and headed back to our room. It was supposed to have been a day of physical and mental rest, yet we were exhausted. We spent more time in the sun and on our feet than we should have, but we didn't regret one single minute of the way we had spent our day. We had been in Africa for less than 24 hours and we already had an amazing experience discovering Moshi and spending time with the children at the orphanage. Pam and I commented to one another that we couldn't imagine what the rest of the trip would be like, as our first 24 hours had been fantastic.

CB

What are you doing to make an emotional connection with your customers? Despite conventional wisdom, most buying decisions begin with a desire to feel a specific emotion. As consumers we may not be fully cognizant of what feeling we are seeking, but our decision to move forward is often driven by our desire to connect with a feeling through the experience or association of the product or service. Can you define how your customer wants to *feel* in relationship to your product or service? It is imperative that you first identify – and then start appealing to – that emotion. Once you do, you will soon be on your way to making more sales.

Emotion Meets Logic

Once a buyer makes the emotional connection, they will then move to justifying the purchase with logic. Knowing that cycle is important because you should immediately follow your emotional appeal with the data, features and benefits that can help your prospect *intellectually justify* that his emotional urge to buy is a smart one. Remember this: appeal first to emotion, and then back it up with logic. In addition to increased sales, an emotionally connected customer will be more interested in seeing you and your business succeed and they will be more likely to refer you to others. Making an emotional connection with customers or prospects also leads to greater consumer insights. This connection will tend to cause people to open up and tell you more – they know you value what they have to say, and they also want to help you be successful. Think about how our experience with Pack for a Purpose and Kilimanjaro Kids Care Orphanage took place. Our desire to continue to support both organizations came from a strong emotional connection to the children, and later to the organizations that support those children. We came home and wanted to verify that what we experienced was indeed the result of the efforts of those organizations. The logic of our future contributions was only made possible due to the emotional connection we first had with the children.

Shut Up and Listen

So, how do you make that emotional connection with your customers or prospects? You start by listening, I mean *really* listening. Do you regularly listen to your customers? Do you truly understand their concerns and needs; what is really beneath the surface? Really listening helps customers feel welcome, comfortable and important in every interaction, whether it's through a phone call, face-to-face conversation or email. On the flip-side, however, there's nothing more insulting than feeling that you're being ignored in a conversation. So when you ask someone a question, you must truly listen to the response rather than formulating your response while the other person is speaking. I am sure you know the type of conversation I am talking about – the kind where your last few words are cut off by the other person jumping in. It is hard to actively listen, while thinking about what you want to say and looking for the moment where you can interrupt. The key is to *ask questions and then just listen*. It sounds so simple, yet it seems to be a lost art. Before you launch into selling mode, take time to understand the other person. Ask questions that will help your customer explain what he or she needs. Once you know that information, it is easy to identify whether your product or service is a good match and whether it will satisfy their wants or needs.

Dare to Care

The other key to make an emotional connection is to display caring for the customer's issues. You need to get to know them better. As much as you may want your customers to be concerned about your success, their primary interest is their own success. If you can provide ideas or suggestions that can help them be more successful or to perform their job easier, it shows you care about them. We are so often focused on selling our product and service, and assuming it will fit the needs of our prospect or customer, that we fail to adequately understand their core issues. And without understanding their core issues, it is difficult to understand whether your product or service can solve those issues. Attempting to sell your prospect or customer something that is not relevant to his or her business (or a problem they are facing), will cause you to automatically lose respect and credibility. This might be the result of assuming your product or service will solve the issue that a client is facing – an issue that you might not have adequately diagnosed. Sometimes it makes sense to turn away business even if your solution or offering may solve *part* of their problem. If your product or service doesn't solve the entire problem, you run the risk of winning the initial business but losing future opportunities. Business people remember salespeople who go out of their way to ensure that they receive the best solution, even if it isn't the salesperson's product or service.

John C. Maxwell's quote "people don't care how much you know until they know how much you care," is at the heart of making an emotional connection with a prospect or customer. Imagine how different an experience it would have been for everyone if Pam and I had showed up at the orphanage focused on what we wanted. Imagine how different it would have been if we spent the time we had at the orphanage talking about our life in Indiana. We received so much more than we gave because our focus was on the children, not on us.

Where is your focus? Is it on your customer's needs or are you focused on your desire to close the deal? Take the time to really get to know the other person. Make an emotional connection. Your customers will be better served, and you will prosper, too.

CHAPTER 8

GIVE ME WHAT
WEIGHS YOU DOWN

When Pam and I made the decision to travel to Tanzania and climb Mount Kilimanjaro, we knew we wouldn't be making the climb alone; but we did not yet know if we would be part of a small or large group. A couple of weeks before our trip we discovered that our group would total 15 participants! We also discovered that our support team would number 13. In other words, Pam and I would be the only tourists or guests on this climb.

At first it was hard to get our heads around the idea that it would take 13 people – a lead guide, assistant guide and 11 porters – to support the climbing efforts of just two first-timers. We soon found out, however, that with all the gear, tents, food, water and other supplies, these 13 experienced assistants would be essential.

Still, we had to wonder: How would being the only guests on the climb impact us? Would we thrive as the focus of our assistants' efforts? Or would we feel extra pressure because of that focus? To be honest, at ages 50 (me) and 49 (Pam), we worried if we could keep up with the group. We didn't want to be "those people". . . you know, the weak links that everyone else must wait on. Our ideal scenario was to be part of a large group whose slowest person would be, well, *someone else.* That scenario, of course, went out the window when we realized the slowest person would indeed *have to be* one of us!

These Are Our Leaders?

We met our lead guide, Haruni (pronounced HA-ROON'), on that Sunday night, at the end of our first full day in Tanzania. Haruni was 34 years old. He stood probably 5' 4" tall (if that), and he was very soft-spoken. Not exactly my idea of the big, strong leader I had imagined would take us up Kili. Because Pam and I were both much taller and weighed quite a bit more than Haruni, I wondered if we would be in capable hands. After all, we were likely only going to have one opportunity to climb this mountain. To accomplish that, we knew we would need the best possible guide to get us to the top.

The next day, at the trailhead, we met Ema (EE'-MAH), our assistant guide. Ema was only 25 years old. (And since our daughter was 24 and our son 21 at the time, we didn't gain much confidence knowing we would be led by someone the age of our kids.) Ema was much taller than Haruni, well over 6 feet, but also very thin. Still, we knew that both Haruni and Ema had made this journey many times; their lack of stature had not diminished their abilities. So, despite our concerns over our leaders, it was looking more and more like we would indeed be the weak links on this team.

Day One – First Signs of Trouble

Day One started on a Monday morning at the mile-high Machame (MA-SHAH'-MAY) Gate (elevation of 1,640 meters, or 5,380 feet) and would end nearly a mile further up at Machame Camp (2,850 meters or 9,350 feet). This was anticipated to be a 6 to 7 hour hike, with a total lineal distance covered of 11 km (7 miles). No easy feat, but we had trained for this and knew that many tougher challenges lie ahead. The first of those challenges hit almost immediately, and within a few hours of starting our ascent I discovered the leadership we could count on from Haruni and Ema.

The hike was going nicely at first, our preparation serving us well. But after about four hours, when we stopped along the trail for lunch, it hit me. I was sick. Really sick. I hadn't been feeling well when we left Machame Gate, but I thought it was just nerves. And yet as I labored over the first couple of bites of the sandwich from my box lunch, I felt like I couldn't eat any more without throwing up. I broke the news to Pam, Haruni and Ema. Thinking that I was already reacting physically to the change in altitude, they encouraged me to eat so that I might feel better. Even though this made sense, I felt so nauseated that I just couldn't bear the thought of taking another bite.

Nearby, a couple of young men were sitting on logs across from us eating their lunches, and they began to offer suggestions. Apparently, it was very easy to see that I wasn't feeling well. I turned to Pam. "I can't believe after all of our training and planning that I might not make it through the first day." Tears welled up in her eyes. I hung my head. I just couldn't fathom that this was happening to me. To us!

If One of Us Can't Go On, the Other Must

Haruni asked if he could help me and I said I didn't think so. In fact, I told him I wasn't sure if I could even continue on. I said I would give it a go, but only if we could proceed very slowly and take frequent breaks. Pam smiled at me, but I could see in her eyes that she was already replaying in her mind our pact. Before arriving in Africa, we had agreed: "If one of us can't go on, the other one must try to reach the summit." We had thought that this possibility would not occur until we were in the later stretches of scaling the mountain, but here it was already. First day. With so little of the journey behind us, so much still ahead.

This is when I learned how important Haruni and his style of servant-leadership would be for us.

With quiet calm and persistent reassurance, Haruni stepped toward me. "Give me some things from your pack," he said. "Give me what weighs you down."

With masculine pride, I tried to shrug off his offer. I told him I didn't have anything that was very heavy. He shook his head and said he would not take "no" for an answer. At his insistence I opened my backpack. I showed him that I had rain pants, a camera and binoculars, along with some other small items. None of these things were what I considered heavy, but together they did add up to maybe 15 pounds.

Let Me Lighten Your Load

Haruni held out his hands, as if to say, "Let me lighten your load." I looked at Pam. Then I looked up the mountain to where the peak lay beyond the shelf of clouds. And I relaxed my shoulders and exhaled heavily, letting down my resistance and letting go of my stubborn ego. Because Haruni, this noble little man, made it very easy to ask for — and accept — his help, I started to hand over some of the items. My backpack became lighter, my load more bearable.

This was the first time Haruni took on some of our burden, but it definitely wouldn't be the last. Throughout our journey, Haruni and Ema were firm and direct with us when our safety was at risk, but mostly they focused on our needs and how they could serve us. We knew they had our best interests at heart, but we also knew who was in charge. From that moment we knew that a successful relationship and a successful adventure would come from trust. So we followed. And as we followed we also listened and learned, confident that with each step, Haruni and Ema, our servant-leaders were bringing us that much closer to our goal: reaching the summit of Mount Kilimanjaro.

CR

There is often a misconception that servant-leaders lose their power or their authority or their ability to lead by focusing on followers first. Quite the contrary; servant-leaders gain followers, earn respect and attract success because of their outward focus. This misconception often stems from not understanding the difference between "service" and "servitude." Servitude implies being in a one-down position to another person and giving from a place of "need to" or "have to." True service, by contrast, stems from a desire to give from the heart. Service is freely shared without any expectation for something in return. The reward gained from service is the sheer joy of giving.

Finding Power in Service

Not only does being a servant-leader not cause you to lose your power, authority or your ability to lead, focusing on others will actually increase revenue! Servant-leadership is powerful because the sales leader is a servant first. This style of "leadership by example" inspires a sales team to do their best because they know their sales manager has their best interests as their primary goal. Remember, your sales team wants to know that their sales leader really cares about them. If you get it right, you will build a highly-functioning sales team, and in turn, find the competitive advantage you have been looking for (Hint: It's been under your nose the whole time: it's your people!).

Servant-leadership can take you and your team on a new and exciting journey. It can help you mend relationships and create a caring and enthusiastic environment that makes it possible to achieve great things (maybe even beyond your wildest dreams). We were only halfway through our first day when I started to encounter trouble. Because it was so early in our journey, I hadn't had a chance to develop a relationship with Haruni and Ema. I didn't know either of them very well. I didn't know what type of leaders they would be. Their humble, service-first approach not only helped me through a really difficult situation, it made me fight for them much harder. I didn't want to let down the people that had already invested so much in me. Did Haruni and Ema lose power, authority or their ability to lead because they were serving? No, very much to the contrary.

Whatever It Takes

If you are a sales leader, dare to be different. Focus on others first. Be the kind of person you want your people to be. Don't ask anything of your team that you aren't willing to do yourself. Be the first person to arrive and the last to leave. Don't be afraid of grunt work (don't look at it as being beneath you). Doing your share of the dirty work clearly demonstrates that you don't place yourself above anyone — or any task — and that you are willing to do whatever it takes to lead a successful team. If you do that, it will be difficult for someone on your sales team to refuse a task in light of your action. "I'm too good for that," won't apply if you, as the sales leader, take your turn.

Servant-leaders are humble: *they don't think less of themselves; they just think about themselves less.* Sales leaders who serve their sales teams are sharply different because their primary interests are not their own priorities; rather they seek to serve the needs of their teams. Sales leaders who act as "servants" actively model how to reach, listen to, and respond to the needs of their team, showing them how they should interact with their clients. It is a cycle. If we prefer to have our leaders serve us, then it would stand to reason that our sales teams want us to serve *them.* It is equally reasonable to assume that our customers want us to serve them; an*d cu*stomers who feel adequately served tend to buy more. That is the purest definition of a win-win-win!

The Starbucks® Example

Howard Behar, former President of Starbucks North America said it best: "*It's Not About the Coffee*" (fittingly, the title of his book). Starbucks was a medium-sized business realizing healthy sales growth when its leaders started to practice servant-leadership. The rest, as they say, is history. Behar helped build Starbucks into the world's largest coffee chain on a culture of customer service and a dedication to servant-leadership. They discovered that by serving customers – truly *serving* them – Starbucks could make deeper connections and earn loyalty along with sales.

The Starbucks model provides another important lesson about servant-leadership: teach your followers how to lead themselves. Toward that goal, former Starbucks CEO Howard Schultz put in motion his belief that you should "surround yourself with great people and get out of the way." Thus, servant-leaders at Starbucks (and in successful companies around the world) set an example guided by core values, and then empower their followers to lead themselves – and others.

Thanks to the servant-leadership of our guides, Pam and I made it to Machame Camp that evening. It took a little longer than expected, but we did make it (I found out later that I had experienced food poisoning). It only took 4 hours of hiking for me to realize how much I appreciated my leaders. How long has it taken for your sales team to realize what type of leader you are? How long has it taken for your customers to realize what type of salesperson you are? More importantly, do you like the answer they came up with?

CHAPTER 9

MAMA AND DADEE

After overcoming food poisoning and a long day, we slogged into our first night's stop: Machame Camp. We were eagerly looking forward to resting in our tent before dinner time; however, before we could shed our backpacks and relax a bit, we were directed to a small hut where the daily protocol was to sign the camp's registration log. The reason for signing in made a great deal of sense – to verify who made it to camp at the end of each day – although it was somewhat disturbing. The rationale behind this daily ritual is to know when someone is missing and identify where they got lost. In other words, if you signed a registration log the day before, but not today, you must be "out there somewhere" on today's trail. I am glad that Pam and I were able to place our names in each day's book!

The register was a large book (approximately 8.5 inches by 17 inches) where you needed to list a great deal of information: your name, age, country, trekking company, guides names, etc. It was after the first day when I realized we were among the oldest "guests" on the mountain. Each page held 30 to 40 names. Pam signed in first and noticed that there wasn't anyone on that page within 10 years of our ages. She commented, "I'm the oldest person on this page!" I then reminded her that after I signed the log she would lose that dubious title. While I would like to tell you that our experience on the first day of this daily ritual was an aberration and that we weren't the oldest people (by a great margin) each day, but that wouldn't be the truth. Before each sign-in we scanned the page we were about to sign, and looked back a page or two. Day after day, no one was even close to our age. Finally, one day we saw someone listed who was in their 40's; we smiled and commented that we had found a kindred spirit.

Turtles and Hares

Pam and I started to have fun with the fact that we were among the oldest on the mountain, and we began to pay more attention to the faces of everyone we saw at camp or that we passed on the trail. During our 7 day trek up and down Kili, we saw only 3 or 4 faces that looked to be our age or older. Apparently this trek was for those in their twenties and thirties, but here we were crashing their party! On more than one occasion we saw a particular young group move by us quickly only to see them an hour or so later, sitting on a rock hunched over and taking an extended break. It wasn't unusual to see this same young group quickly move by us once more only to find them "resting" as we again trudged by. When we stopped seeing some of those young groups again, Pam and I figured they must have needed to turn around and head back down the mountain. The more sensible approach, we had read (and were often reminded by our guides), is to move slowly – pole' pole' – (PO-lay PO-lay), and we heeded that advice. So it didn't take long for us to realize that we were a 21st century version of the turtle and the hare. Whenever we saw a group of younger climbers move past us more quickly than they should, Pam and I would just nod in their direction and say one word to one another: "Hare."

New Names, Smarter Approach

When we met Haruni the evening before our climb started, we had introduced ourselves as Pam and Mark. The next morning when we met Ema and the rest of our crew, we quickly became known as "Mama" and "Dadee." At first, we were a little taken aback, but we realized that many in our crew (including Ema) were the ages of our children or younger. We understood these names were bestowed with affection, and we quickly embraced and cherished them and began to call each other by our new names!

Being amongst the oldest trekkers on the mountain inherently meant that we had a greater challenge ahead of us, but it was a challenge that began to drive us. We not only didn't fear that age would prevent us from reaching the summit, we decided to turn that *obstacle* into an *opportunity*. We began to think about how much sweeter it would be to make it to the top of Kilimanjaro at our age — to reach the summit at twice the age of many of the climbers. But we had so much mountain left to climb, and at these high altitudes we knew we couldn't rely only on brute strength; we would need to be *smarter*.

Knowing that we had a smaller margin of error than younger climbers, we felt like we could make up for no longer having youthful exuberance by paying attention to details. We quizzed Haruni and Ema each day about proper pace, how best to prepare for each day, when to eat and drink and how much rest was needed. We knew the "older version of us" would pay attention to every detail, when the "younger version of us" might just think we could outwork the mountain. I was reminded of older professional athletes who had perhaps lost a step or two but were still very competitive because they utilized the knowledge and experience that comes from age. Being "past our prime," I wasn't sure we could compete at a world-class level like Jerry Rice or Dara Torres did in their forties, but like them, I felt we would have a better story to tell when we succeeded.

We found ourselves focusing on the joy of keeping up with

61

groups much younger than us, and not on why age might be a limitation. We thought back to when we started to plan for this trip and how we liked the idea of being those "crazy people." We talked often about not only being the "crazy people" that attempted to climb Kilimanjaro, but being part of the 43% that actually made it to the summit. The odds were clearly against us, but we knew we had trained as hard as people half our age and that we were ready. Finding out we were among the oldest on the mountain turned into a real blessing. We were already motivated, but the fact that you could count the people on the mountain that were older than us on one hand, really brought smiles to our faces. Could we really pull this off? The possibility was pretty awesome to consider.

☙

In Benjamin Zander's book, *The Art of Possibility*, he tells the story of two shoe salesmen who were sent to Africa. After checking out the territory, one writes back by telegram, "No one in Africa wears shoes. I'm coming home." The other salesman writes back by telegram, "No one in Africa wears shoes. Send the whole sales team!" The former salesman saw the obstacle; the latter saw the opportunity.

In the same way the salesmen in Africa made a determination on whether the lack of African people wearing shoes was an obstacle or opportunity, you also have the power to decide on the impact of what you are facing. I believe this: when we are given the opportunity to face a challenge, we have a chance to show our character. We have the power to decide how we will handle it. Traditional sales training programs often ignore the biggest obstacles to success. The biggest obstacles are usually not related to sales talent, motivation or knowledge of techniques. Rather, the biggest obstacles are often the internal, mental, and emotional barriers that sales professionals face on a daily basis. Don't let the obstacles that come up in your sales career cause you to lose sight of your goals. Being one of the oldest climbers on Kilimanjaro that week could have been an obstacle for

Pam and me, but we chose to focus on the excitement we would surely feel when reaching the summit at our ages. We focused on the goal, not the obstacle. Think of the obstacles you face as chances to grow. Take a deep breath, stick out your chest, and take on the challenge.

Overcoming Obstacles and Objections on Your Way to the Top

Ultimately, how you handle an obstacle defines you. Are you weak? Are you a quitter? Or are you strong? Will you endure through hard times? When an obstacle is put in your way, it is up to you to find a way around it. Getting food poisoning on the first day of our trek wasn't what I wanted to have happen, but it did make success all the more sweet. So, when you face a major obstacle – a crucial moment in your life – you only have two options: Crumble or Conquer. Don't give up and sidestep the challenge. Realize that *everyone* faces obstacles; the difference is how you handle the situation. Be the better person. Be a conqueror. Let life know you're a *machine!*

Henry Ford once said, "Whether you think you can, or you think you can't – you're right." We often achieve what we focus on. Focus on the obstacle and you will almost certainly fail. Focus on the goal and you will more likely succeed. The destination we keep in sight is usually where we end up.

With this in mind, think about sales objections. First, understand that a sales objection is NOT a "no!" Rather, it is an opportunity to communicate more; an opportunity to move the prospect to the next stage in your sales process. I have found that an objection is usually one of three things:

1. *A hidden indicator of interest.* Objections show some level of interest and enable the salesperson to give more information to the prospect. The more information the prospect has, the easier it is to make the sale.

2. *A request for more information.* Many salespeople hear the prospect saying "No," when what they are really saying is,

"You haven't given me enough of a compelling reason to buy from you," or, "You haven't satisfied all of my concerns and priorities."

3. *A concern or fear.* This gives you the opportunity to satisfy a real – even if not clearly expressed – sense of anxiety, so you can continue guiding the buyer through your sales process and to its natural conclusion.

Objections, after all, are a natural part of the selling process. If there are no objections, it could mean that the prospect is apathetic. Instead of fearing objections, embrace them! Indeed, after you have overcome an obstacle you will likely feel a large weight lifted off your shoulders. You become a new person with newfound confidence and a new drive. Doesn't that sound much better than being one of *those people* who always have problems hovering over them simply because they are afraid to take them on? It sure does to me.

Keeping the Summit in Sight

Most salespeople have the tools to be successful and I would imagine most of the hikers that attempt to climb Kilimanjaro are physically ready. Where it gets interesting is when a prospect's budget is reduced or when the oxygen in the atmosphere gets thinner. It is in that environment of adversity that our character is revealed. Do we focus on how much more difficult it will be to attain our sales quota, or do we get excited knowing most salespeople will quit while we are working on a creative way to exceed our quota? Do we focus on how much harder it is to breathe, or do we get excited knowing that less oxygen means we are getting really close to the summit? The only difference is your perspective.

CHAPTER 10

A DAILY ROUTINE THAT
WASN'T VERY ROUTINE

I 'll be honest – it was hard to get my mind around what it would be like to climb to the top of the highest freestanding mountain in the world. I couldn't quite imagine what climbing to 19,341 feet would feel like or how difficult it would be. In anticipation of our trip, we watched videos on YouTube and witnessed much younger people near the top of Kilimanjaro breathing so heavily that it was difficult for them to talk. Every time Pam and I thought about the difficulty of climbing to that high altitude, we got a bit anxious and started to doubt ourselves. Not surprisingly, we found this to be true on the actual trek up Kilimanjaro as well. We found that when we were able to catch a glimpse of the peak while on the trail, it looked so far away. *Too* far away to actually reach.

One Step at a Time

To make the summit reachable, we knew that we needed to shift our focus from the overall goal to the *process* of the ascent – to our daily routine. We knew it would take us 5 ½ days to get to the top, so it didn't make sense to worry about getting to the top on Day One or Day Two. We also learned that such thoughts – such *anxiety* – could only work against us.

I remember when a friend convinced me to run a half marathon for the first time. He and I went out four months before the race for our first run and I found myself demoralized because I couldn't make it a half mile without walking. I couldn't imagine what would be like to run 13.1 miles. I felt that anxiousness again when I considered running a full marathon after I finished my second half marathon. I had just finished running 13.1 miles and I began to think what it would be like to turn around and run all the way back to the start line. What I found during my training is that I needed to only focus on what I needed to run that day – and what I needed to run that week. It was essential that I stick with the plan and slowly increase the distances I ran. If I stuck with the plan, I would get to the point where I was ready to run those full distances. Climbing Kilimanjaro was much the same. We needed to focus only on what we were going to hike that day; and more importantly, we broke each day into smaller segments. We trusted that if we followed the routine that had been set out for us, we would indeed make it to the top of Kilimanjaro.

Cadence of the Days

Each day had cadence to it. A series of events that occurred every morning, afternoon and evening. Haruni and Ema put the events in motion, and within that overall framework, Pam and I put our own spin on each day. Our days began with Iddi (our "waiter") waking us each morning, crouching outside our tent and hearing his soft-spoken voice calling "Ma-maah, Da-deee," until we responded, "Iddi! Good morning!" He had the gentlest spirit and the warmest smile you could ever imagine. He was excited to serve us coffee and tea each morning. To this day, Pam and I still speak fondly of Iddi, and often call each other "Mama" and "Dadee" in the same excited voice that he used. Iddi would also place two bowls of water — one hot, one cold — with a small travel-sized bar of white soap outside of our tent and he would point at the bowls and say "water for washing." Believe me; with the amount of dust that covered everything around you, "water for washing" brought a smile to our faces each day. We got used to eating breakfast proudly served by Iddi in our "mess tent" and having Haruni show up at the end of the meal to take our vital signs, reaffirm what we should wear, and give us some insight into what that day would hold for us. Between breakfast and the time we headed out from camp, we knew we needed to pack up our sleeping bag, clothes, and other items into our duffel bags and leave them in our tent for the porters to carry. We brought our camelbacks to breakfast, and Iddi would take and fill them with hot water that had just been boiled. Ema led us out from camp each day, while Haruni would stay back to supervise the breakdown of our campsite and to make sure each porter was carrying the right amount of weight. We quickly learned what was expected, and we trusted the process.

Each day Haruni would catch up with us after an hour or so. We were amazed daily that the porters who stayed behind to pack up camp were soon passing us as if we were standing still! We would hear voices and quick footsteps behind us and then we would hear "Jambo, Mama! Dadee!" And our entourage would blow past us! When we arrived at the next camp, all would be ready for our arrival. They were superheroes as they moved quickly past us, carrying 30 to 40 lbs. on their backs and/or on top their heads. We looked forward to eating the boxed lunches Ema carried each day in his backpack. We were given more to eat than we could often consume and then we found out that the porters only received one meal per day. We felt embarrassed and privileged at the same time. We didn't want to waste this extra food, so what we didn't eat we gave to Haruni and Ema and they would offer our extra food to the porters.

Tea and Popcorn

Most days, we hiked for 7 to 10 hours. Near the end of each day as the sun began to fall, we started to look ahead for "tent city." Tent city was the 100+ tents we would see in the distance, signaling that the end of our hiking day was near. Because we would "hike high and sleep low," we could usually see our camping location well below us, and it would take an hour or so from the time we first saw camp to when we arrived. At the end of a long day on the trail, it was almost like a mirage, but finally we would walk into camp, sign the registry book and find our duffel bags placed side by side inside our tent. We then inflated our air mattresses, put our sleeping bags in place and readied ourselves for afternoon tea and popcorn. Iddi would crouch beside our tent and say in that all familiar voice, "tea and popcorn," and that was our cue to come to the tent where we would eat our meals. The popcorn selection varied each day. One day it was sprinkled with sugar – like kettle corn, and the next it was mixed with roasted Spanish peanuts. After a long day of hiking, tea and popcorn was as good as filet mignon and the finest red wine!

After tea and popcorn, we typically had another hour to relax before dinner. Iddi would bring us the "water for washing" a few minutes before dinner was served. Haruni would join us about halfway through the meal, and always insisted that we eat more food. The higher we climbed, the poorer our appetite became, and he encouraged us to eat as much as possible in order to help avoid altitude sickness. Haruni briefed us on what the next day's travel would consist of and he would once again take our vital signs to verify that we were doing well. We brought our 1-liter Nalgene bottles to dinner each night to be filled with hot water. This bottle was not only the source of our morning drinking water, but the reason our feet stayed warm each night. The sun sets very early near the equator, and it was typically pitch black by the time dinner was over. It was usually around 7:00 p.m. when we headed to our tent. The mountainside was lit by the moon and stars and the scattered headlamps glowing inside many of the tents.

We would spend the next hour the same way each night. We immediately placed the first purification pill in our water bottles, and then added the second pill 30 minutes later. After settling deep into our sleeping bags with our headlamps on, we journaled about the day's events. We wrote about what we saw each day, but mostly, we wrote about our amazing team and the kindness of the African people. Due to the amount of water and tea we consumed each day, one last trip to the toilet tent was needed, and I quickly learned that turning off your headlamp while inside brought much less attention to yourself! We fell asleep each night around 8:00 p.m. to the sounds of our team laughing in the main tent and talking in Swahili.

This daily routine became ordinary; yet it wasn't a routine we had ever followed before. Still, we clung to it each day, knowing that if we followed the process, we would be successful. We didn't have to climb all 19,341 feet in one day; we just needed to wake up to Iddi calling "Mama" and "Dadee," follow what our guides told us to do during the day, and then fall asleep to the joyful sound of our team laughing (not at us, we hoped!). It became not only the way we would scale Kilimanjaro, it became the way we would get the most out of every day.

ନ୍ଧ

Top salespeople don't "wing it" anymore. The days of walking into your office and pounding the phones are gone. You are not just selling; you are strategizing on growing your territory. You are managing a virtual team to support your efforts, learning new tools, and incorporating them into your sales process. You are reaching out via email, networking through social media tools, conducting webinars and selling through strategic partners. Most of us have routines. We get up at the same time each workday, follow a regular pattern of shower, coffee, morning news and then our commute, with little deviation from one day to the next. And that's the way it should be with sales as well. You shouldn't be in the position of "reinventing the wheel" every time you engage a client. If you have a routine and it isn't working, you will have a better idea of what to change. If you don't have a routine, how do you know what isn't working? You haven't done anything on a consistent basis; thus, you can't identify the problem. If you treat your sales process like Haruni treated a day on the mountain, your "summit" won't be too far away.

Silencing the Alarm

Because our brains are built to sound the alarm when confronted with an enormous sales goal, we need to adjust our expectations so our alarm doesn't go off. We need to set smaller sales goals that feel more reasonable and sustainable. These smaller goals are merely different facets of our overall target; sometimes they are identical, measured increments of the big sales goal. When Pam and I looked up to the summit thousands of feet above us and allowed our minds to wander to the difficulty of the climb, we because anxious. We knew we needed to get back to thinking about only the day's climb, perhaps making it to lunch time or maybe just over the next ridge. In the same way, you need to do something daily to get you closer to your sales goal. As you work on your daily goals, they get you closer toward the bigger goal. But you need to be willing to adapt. Make the small goals more difficult if they seem too easy. Make them easier if they become too taxing. The main thing is that if your small goals are too difficult, you'll quit. If they are too easy, you're running in place. Find the middle, so you truly advance toward your ultimate goal each day.

Munching on Elephants

Even though you have divided your overall goal into manageable, smaller goals, it can still be a long journey. I knew that the end of each day on the slopes of Kilimanjaro meant I had accomplished a smaller goal and that I was closer to the overall goal of reaching the summit. Sometimes it felt like I still had a long way to go — and early in the trip, I did. I needed to reward myself for getting through the end of the day or for making it to the top of a ridge. My rewards ranged from looking ahead to what tomorrow had in store for us - to having tea and popcorn and a short nap - to a water break. Each of those "rewards" reaffirmed that I had done well. We need that in sales too. We need to reward ourselves along the way. Take time to enjoy your hard work and effort. We would all like to think that we work as hard as we can all the time . . . but that isn't always the truth. Reward yourself along the way and you'll have more of an incentive to reach your sales goal. The reward can be something small, but make it meaningful. The point is this: if you know you get a reward at steps along the way, you'll continue to be fired up! Reward yourself for doing what you told yourself that you'd do. Reward yourself even when others don't.

While keeping your eye on your goal is important, it can often be overwhelming. If you dream big, the effort to achieve that dream is also big. It doesn't matter if your goal is scaling Kilimanjaro or if it is growing your territory 40% over last year; it takes a series of smaller steps to get there. If you don't know what those smaller steps are, you are going to have to wing it. Dreaming big isn't scary, but "winging it" is!

Remember the answer to the old saying "how do you eat an elephant?" *One bite at a time!* So dream big, break your goal into smaller steps and reward yourself along the way. You just might find yourself on top of the world, looking down from the summit of your achievement.

CHAPTER 11

MONITOR YOUR PERFORMANCE

It was after dinner on Day One when I really began to appreciate the complexity of scaling Kilimanjaro. I had just been through a difficult day and was starting to feel a bit better after we arrived at Machame Camp. I was able to lie down for a little while and gain back some of the strength I had lost from the effects of the food poisoning. As Day One wore on, I was feeling rather weak and shaky. I had eaten very little at lunchtime, and while I did my best to stay hydrated during the day, I knew that I had fallen short on water intake. The unexpected surprise of tea and popcorn when we arrived at camp did make my empty stomach feel better, but I was still somewhat depleted from the day's events. Proper eating and drinking on the hike was vitally important, so I was a concerned about getting off to such a poor start.

Long before we boarded our flight out of Indianapolis, we had done a lot of research and discovered that only 43% of those climbing Kilimanjaro actually make it to the summit. Obviously, we did not want to be part of the 57% that didn't make it. We had learned that hikers typically fail because of some combination of four factors: the high altitude, a too-fast rate of ascent, a high degree of exertion and/or dehydration. Armed with this knowledge, it had been our intent to get off to a good start. Day One is arguably the easiest day of the hike, even though we had climbed nearly 4,000 feet that day. By the time we reached Machame Camp we were still at a relatively low altitude of 9,350 feet, although that was definitely a lot higher than hiking 817 feet back home in Indiana! But despite our best efforts to learn what to do and what *not* to do, I had violated – at least to some degree – all four of the main reasons people do not reach the summit: I didn't eat or drink as much as I should have that first day, I was still getting used to the altitude, and we were ascending at a rate faster than what my body wanted to go, albeit because of the food poisoning.

Testing Begins

Following dinner on Day One, we learned that we would be participating in an after-dinner ritual to help us identify if our bodies were handling the hike well and if we were in good enough shape to continue. It was comforting to know that Haruni and Ema would be watching our health so closely, yet disconcerting to feel that a test would determine if we could go on. I was even more concerned because I definitely did not feel my best after a rough first day. I wasn't sure I wanted to see my results. Every morning after breakfast and every evening after dinner, Haruni would use an oximeter to test our blood oxygen saturation level and our pulse rate. An oximeter is a clip-on finger device that measures the percentage of oxygen-rich red blood cells that travel through your body. The range you can score is from 0-100. My first reading was a 93 and Pam's reading was an 86. Haruni told us those were good scores, so I began to feel better about my situation. Pam was a little worried that her score wasn't higher than mine – given the fact that I was the one who didn't feel well! I was pretty sure I didn't deserve the good score, but I sure was going to take it! Fortunately, I began to regain my appetite and ate a decent amount of food that evening. Haruni told us that as we climbed higher, we should expect our readings to drop due to the altitude and likely confront some form of acclimatization issues.

In addition to using an oximeter, our health was monitored in other ways. Haruni and Ema paid attention to our stamina, our appetite, our water intake, our communications (slurring words, etc.), our breathing, and if we had headaches or other symptoms. They asked us often how we were feeling.

That first night Haruni addressed the importance of eating well. He mentioned that on Days One and Two we would likely have our best appetites. He told us that we would need to be sure to eat well, because we would need to keep our strength up as the higher altitude put more stress on our bodies. This would be especially important as we neared the summit. Our dinners typically consisted of rice mixed with beans or meat, or some type of pasta. Bread, fruit and vegetables were served with each meal. We needed plenty of carbohydrates to keep up our energy levels.

A Different Kind of Dehydration

Hydration, of course, was always a concern. We each carried three liters of water inside our camelbacks and an extra one-liter water bottle in an outside pocket on our backpacks. Haruni and Ema stopped often to remind us to drink; and Pam and I tried to remind each other to drink from our camelbacks whenever it had been a while since the last water stop or after going through difficult terrain. I commented to Pam at the end of Day Two that we started the day drinking a couple of cups of hot tea and then had four liters of water during the hike, yet we didn't go to the bathroom all day. Staying hydrated at high altitude was a much different experience for us. You get used to how much you sweat and how much you need to drink when you exercise at home; but your body reacts quite differently at high altitude. Dehydration is more likely at altitude because the decreased air pressure makes you breathe deeper and faster. I tried to remind myself of the old adage "by the time you get thirsty, you're already dehydrated." It was also much more difficult to monitor how hard our bodies were working because our training had taken place during warmer weather. Because it got much colder after the first day, it was more difficult to know how much we were sweating.

Before embarking on our adventure, we had read another troubling fact: At points over 10,000 feet, more than 75% of climbers experience at least some form of mild Acute Mountain Sickness (AMS). We passed 10,000 feet early on the second day. We also knew that at high altitude we would only have 50% of normal oxygen levels. We paid close attention to our guides, knowing that they were experienced in identifying AMS and helping climbers deal with the problems it causes. We also knew it was important to be open and honest with our guides about how we felt. We didn't want our health to prevent us from getting to the summit, but we knew the consequences of AMS if ignored. So we were on the lookout for any hangover-like symptoms – headache, nausea, and fatigue – because we knew that these signs of AMS could be a gateway to more serious forms of altitude sickness that can cause fluid on the lungs, fluid on the brain, and eventually, death.

Even though Pam and I felt certain that we would know if we were struggling and our health was deteriorating, we were comfortable knowing that Haruni and Ema knew what signs to look for and were constantly monitoring our performance and health.

CR

With our health potentially at risk, it isn't hard to understand why monitoring our vital signs on Kilimanjaro was important and why a close watch on food consumption and hydration was in order. But is sales really that different? Life and death might not hang in the balance, but your "sales health" can be at risk if unmonitored. You can't rely on hope and assumptions; you need to have timely and accurate information about your sales performance. You must assess real data in *real time* so it will reveal current conditions. Armed with this information, you can take immediate action before it is too late.

Being Productive on the Right Activities

You may be staying busy and giving 100% effort every day, but that doesn't mean you are being productive. Find a way to quantify your performance. Make sure you are giving your best effort toward the right activities. Good sales data may cause you to change your behavior so your efforts are not wasted. Once you understand the activities you should focus on, you can devote more time and energy to these areas. Ultimately, it will help you make better decisions.

Understanding our blood pressure and blood oxygen level were not only Key Performance Indicators (KPIs), they were also useful because they were *leading indicators* – signposts along the way that we were doing the things we needed to do in order to be successful. What are your KPIs? Identify and track the KPIs that will provide you with the visibility into your current activity that will also impact future sales productivity. Tracking these KPIs (also known as, simply, *indicators*) in the present will allow you to identify gaps and help you influence the outcomes of those monthly, quarterly and annual productivity numbers that are so important. You must also differentiate between leading indicators and *lagging* indicators. Leading indicators attempt to identify future events that signal growth or contraction; lagging indicators report on data that comes from past activity. The proper mix of each type of indicator is important if you want to be able to measure results and predict outcomes.

What Should You Measure?

Conventional wisdom holds that the only important measure is revenue produced; but I believe other metrics also need to be tracked. Here is my short list:

- **Opportunity Pipeline** – this dollar amount indicates the sales expected in future periods (month/quarter/year).

This metric is dynamic and will keep changing as new opportunities come in and old opportunities move out.

- **Sales Mix** – you need to understand the source of your revenue. Examples include account type (new and existing), market segment (products and services), geography (region and country), and channel (direct and indirect).

- **Cost of Sales to Revenue Ratio** – this ratio measures sales efficiency by comparing sales costs as a proportion of total revenue. This ratio should include salaries, commissions and expenses for sales management, salespeople and sales support. Are you paying too much for each dollar of revenue?

- **Conversion Rates and Ratios** – these metrics are very useful in identifying process issues like the percentage of qualified opportunities that are won, the percentage of deals that don't close after receiving a proposal, and the percentage of qualified opportunities that show no movement over a period of time.

- **Gross Margin Percentage** – this key metric measures the sales team's performance, by not only looking at total revenue, but also the quality of each individual sale.

Monitoring your sales performance is a lot like monitoring your body on Kilimanjaro. If you put your head down and work hard, you will likely find yourself much further along the path than when you started. To make sure you are progressing on the *right* path, you'll need to know what performance to measure while learning from the wisdom of those who have traveled the path before you. Your "sales health" will benefit from knowing you have the proper pipeline levels for each product offering, in the same way that your body's health will benefit from knowing that you have the proper blood oxygen saturation level. Working hard is great. Working smart is even better.

CHAPTER 12

EMA IS DEAD?

It was only a couple years ago that Pam and I became "empty-nesters" and began to reconnect as a couple. You spend so much time in the role of Mom and Dad that sometimes you can lose sight of your role as Wife and Husband. I remember sitting across the dinner table from Pam the day our son went to college, leaving us with no kids at home, and asking her, "So, what have you been doing for the last 23 years?" It was at that point we began to understand that on a daily basis "Team Thacker" was once again just the two of us. We missed our kids a lot and we looked forward to seeing them whenever possible, but the thought of what our world might look like with just the two of us was exciting! "Signing up for a sculpting class" became the humorous mantra we used to describe what we could do with our rediscovered freedom. We laughed every time we said it, because we knew that our future was limited only by our imaginations. We didn't have an endless amount of time or money, but we knew that many of life's adventures could be had with some advance planning and commitment. It was that thought process that led to our trip to Australia and New Zealand, and ultimately to the bucket list that included climbing Mount Kilimanjaro.

Finding Focus

I hate to admit it, but in the past I was sometimes "that guy" on vacation who took his laptop with him and did more work than he should. I wanted to get completely away from the corporate rat race, but often I couldn't resist the urge to check email daily, respond to just a few, and participate on an occasional conference call. For that reason I really looked forward to climbing Kilimanjaro. I read that there is occasional cell phone service on the mountain, but I was pretty sure I wasn't going to have access to any cell phone charger. I read about solar battery chargers online and I even saw one at REI, but I resisted the urge to make this vacation like every other vacation over the past 20 years. I began to embrace the concept of "getting off the grid." I knew that with my phone off the entire day, I could truly enjoy the journey ahead – and that's exactly what I did: no client calls, no voicemail, no emails, no social media. Yes, we were able to check for emergency messages periodically, but barring anything catastrophic, there was a backup plan for everything that might happen at home or at work. Life would go on for a week without my involvement.

Freed from normal distractions while hiking for 7 to 10 hours a day gave me the opportunity to focus on Pam, Haruni, Ema and the many other people who crossed our paths. There were times when I needed to keep my head down and watch my step, but most of the time I could look up at our beautiful surroundings and fully engage with my traveling companions. When I am in my normal, day-to-day environment, I would like to tell you that my entire focus is on the words of the person in front of me or that I always observe what is happening around me; but the truth is that my attention is often fragmented. This trip was different. The goal of each day in Tanzania was the same as it is back home: get the most out of each day and enjoy life to the fullest. The difference in getting the most out of each day on Kilimanjaro was not to pack in as much "stuff" as possible; it was to *take in the moment* and enjoy this once-in-a-lifetime experience.

Journaling the Unforgettable

We decided to journal about our trip. After dinner each night we would go back to our tent, burrow into our sleeping bags, and write about that day's amazing adventure. We wrote not only about our experiences, but more importantly, we wrote about what we were thinking and feeling throughout the day. As an example: Referring to the first day when I wasn't sure I could continue after lunch, I wrote "Pam prayed for me and that was a powerful moment." At the end of the fourth day, I wrote about how difficult the day was, finishing my thoughts with, "There's no certificate for first place, only if you finish … God willing, we will." I also kept a section on what I learned, writing about the guides and porters on our team: "I learned that these people make less than one-half of one percent of what I make, work harder than I do, and are more giving than I am." This daily reflection allowed me to relive what was special about each day, and it has continued to provide me with a reminder of the wonderful moments we experienced.

Poor, Poor Ema!

I felt connected to every part of the experience. We spent a lot of time each day with Haruni and Ema and we got to know them really well. They shared stories about their lives, their families and what was important to them. We discovered they had the same sense of humor we did, and we were constantly laughing and joking around. One of my favorite experiences of the entire trip occurred one evening after dinner during our daily oximeter testing. After dinner on the second night, Haruni and Ema joined us to provide a briefing of the next day, as they did nightly. The first evening, Haruni took only the vital signs for Pam and me; but on the second night he also took the vitals for both he and Ema. Each night I wrote the results down in the back my journal, keeping track of our progress. Since Haruni and Ema were now joining us for this daily activity, Haruni encouraged me to keep track of their vital signs as well. We would stick out our index finger and Haruni would clip the oximeter over our fingertip. We would wait for the digital readout, comment on how positive they were, and then I would note the results in my journal. It would normally take 5 to 10 seconds for the oximeter to register and display the information.

On the second night, however, there was trouble getting Ema's results. The oximeter timed out three times after not registering the results after 15 seconds. On the fourth attempt, we finally got results for Ema. After breakfast the next day, we went through the same exercise. Pam, Haruni and I were all able to get results back quickly and the oximeter once again struggled to display Ema's results on the first or second try. We began to laugh about how difficult it was for Ema to get any results. We wondered if it was because he was well over 6' tall and very lean. Ema said he had never had any issues getting results in the past, so we suggested that he try a different finger to see if that would help. No such luck. After dinner on the third night it happened again. The funny part was that Ema was undoubtedly the youngest and healthiest among us, yet his results would not display. I commented to Haruni that something must be wrong with Ema, saying, "Ema must be very, very sick." Haruni began laughing and replied, "Yes, Ema must be very sick." As the laughter continued and Ema still struggled to get a digital readout, I looked at Ema and stated, "I think you may be dead." That caused Haruni to laugh uncontrollably. He pointed at Ema, exclaiming, "Dadee says you are dead!" Poor Ema, we must have repeated, "Ema is dead" a dozen times, laughing harder each time we said it. We laughed so hard that my face and side began to ache. It was the kind of laughter where you badly want to stop laughing – because it hurts! – but you are so tickled that you (and those around you) simply have no control.

Our laughter was contagious. It was a bonding experience, too. After we went back to our tents, still chuckling about "Poor Ema," Pam and I reflected on how awesome it was that people from different continents separated by an ocean and 8,000+ miles – people who live in totally different cultures – are able to find common ground through shared laughter. Suffice it to say that Pam, Haruni and I looked forward to getting our vital signs checked twice each day much more than Ema did. Ema continued to struggle getting his results, and each time we commented that he must be dead – all the while laughing as though it were the first time it had been said. Poor Ema. *Poor, poor Ema!*

CƆ

Identifying the moments in your career that you most enjoy is a lot like identifying what made our Kilimanjaro trip so enjoyable. Too start, eliminating the distractions on our trip up the mountain allowed me to focus on what was important. So, what's important to you? What's a distraction? A sales career isn't for everyone; it can be tough at times, with a lot of travel, time spent away from home, uncertain income, and your performance posted where the whole company can see it. However, it can also be a very rewarding career offering unlimited earning potential, flexible work schedules, job security and an opportunity to make a real difference. What is it about sales that *you* find appealing? I want to share with you a few of the reasons I have enjoyed a career in sales.

25 Mountains

There are 25 mountains in the world that are over 16,300 feet. Kilimanjaro happens to be #4 on that list. I could spend the rest of my life trying to climb the great mountains of the world and likely never reach every peak. A sales career is similar, because your income potential is unlimited. There are very few careers that offer that opportunity. In addition to your salary, you can earn performance rewards in the form of commissions, bonuses, trips and prizes. Not only do you have unlimited earning potential, you are paid solely based on your performance – your compensation is not set in stone; *you* decide how much you make. Therefore, you can give yourself a raise! (If you want to make more, all you have to do is sell more.) Let's face it: nothing happens until something is sold. Successful companies recognize this and that is why good salespeople make a lot of money.

Salespeople also enjoy a flexible work schedule. While the amount of flexibility ranges from job to job, most companies allow sales professionals to set their daily schedules, as long as the specified activity is met. Sales performance typically outweighs hours worked. Getting to the summit is a lot like a salesperson's schedule: Does it matter how hard you worked to get to the top, or does it matter more that you *made it to the top?* Does it matter how many hours it took to attain your quota, or does it only matter that you *reached your destination* (your quota)? If you were to offer a successful salesperson a full-time desk job, you'd probably have your offer rejected. Why? Because once you've enjoyed the freedom of setting your own daily schedule, it is very hard to perform in any job that has the rigid time and location expectations that most office or desk jobs demand.

Satisfaction, Security, Success

You will never take away someone's satisfaction of getting to the summit of Kilimanjaro and you will never take away the job security a good or great salesperson feels. Consider this: Who else in the organization can prove that they "pay for themselves?" It's almost universally true that the last employees to be cut from a struggling business are salespeople; and the last salesperson to be cut is the highest-performing salesperson. Reducing the size of a sales team means cutting incoming revenue, which is not a good plan for a business to remain viable.

I have enjoyed a sales career that provided me with an opportunity for unlimited earnings, flexible work schedules and greater security; but the greatest gift I received as a salesperson was the ability to make a difference in someone's life. The ability to sell a product that can change lives is a great feeling. Many salespeople enjoy knowing that their organization's products and services have a direct and positive impact on the well-being of others. This impact can be felt by a customer and it can also be felt by your employer. Sales is one of the few careers that consistently allows professionals to point to concrete accomplishments. The results of a salesperson's work efforts are clearly measurable, and the benefit that a salesperson brings to an organization can be well-defined. It is similar to reaching the peak of Kilimanjaro – you either climbed to 19,341 feet or you didn't – the results are clear to all.

Life is too short to be stuck in a career you don't enjoy. Being in the wrong career is a lot like being on vacation and not disconnecting from work. You can go through the motions and have an enjoyable time, but you will never truly find joy. Making it to the top of Kilimanjaro would be fulfilling, but taking in all that Tanzania offers is another story. Making true connections with people that will last a lifetime is different than just crossing a trip off a bucket list. With the proper training, and a bit of good fortune, most people can summit Kilimanjaro, but not everyone will walk away from the experience a changed person. I will forget many elements of our trip, but I will never forget the people – they are now my *friends*. Are you performing a job, or are you fulfilling your life's calling? Are you getting the most out of the experience? Are you laughing so hard that your side hurts? It's up to you.

CHAPTER 13

SURROUND YOURSELF WITH A GOOD TEAM

U pon our arrival at the Machame Gate on the first day of our hike we were amazed to learn that 13 others would accompany us as our support team. Thirteen people for just Pam and me?! In addition to Haruni and Ema, we would have a cook, waiter, toilet man and eight porters. Why so many? Because there was a weight limit of 15 kg (32 lbs.) that each porter could carry. Not only did the tents need to be carried, but so did a week's supply of food, water, cooking supplies and all the other items needed to maintain camp. In addition, the porters would carry our duffel bags, which carried all the supplies that we didn't take with us in our backpacks each day. We soon learned that this was a finely tuned team that had worked together often and really enjoyed each other's company.

We didn't realize that we had reserved a portable toilet to be taken up the mountain, so two additional people were needed to carry the small plastic toilet and the tent that surrounded it. Haruni hired those two additional team members the morning we left from the Machame Gate. There is typically a large group of men that come to the Machame Gate each day hoping to be hired for the week. While it wasn't our intent to have this toilet brought with us, we were happy that we were partially responsible for two additional people being hired. And as primitive as it was, it was a definite luxury on the mountain! Because most of the team worked together on a regular basis, they understood their own responsibilities, as well as the responsibilities of other team members. It reminded me a lot of an American football team: each player knew their role in order to make the team successful. The porters took on the role of offensive linemen, in that they provided much of the foundational work that was the backbone of the team. Haruni was the Head Coach, directing the activities of the team and being ultimately responsible for our mission. Ema was the Quarterback who orchestrated the plays that he and Haruni thought needed to be carried out. It was interesting to watch these "well-choreographed plays" take place each morning and afternoon while we were in camp.

"Toilet Man" and the Joyful, Attentive Team

Much like any team, everyone's role was important. We spent most of our time with Haruni and Ema, and we saw Iddi early in the morning, at breakfast and dinner. The other members of our team operated more in the background. We saw some of them occasionally walking around camp, but most often they were behind the scenes. Nonetheless, we were so appreciative of each member of the team, from those we saw often – like Iddi with his huge smile and wonderful servant's heart – to those we saw but once each day. One young man who most impressed us was referred to as the "toilet man." You can imagine his role. Going to the bathroom might be part of life, but in attending to the cleanup and disposal for others he handled his responsibilities with a grace that would be tough to replicate. We often felt guilty having so many people serve us. We didn't feel worthy of having so many heavily invested in our journey. We knew it was their jobs and they were getting paid, but it was difficult to get used to allowing people to help you, knowing that we are normally self-sufficient. Perhaps that was part of what we were supposed to learn. Our team also made it much easier to accept their hospitality due to how joyfully they went about their work.

There were times when we needed to request additional help. Our third day of hiking was one of those times. The higher we climbed up the mountain, the more difficult it became to find a flat spot to set up our tent. At the end of our third day on the mountain, we entered camp to see our tent already up – as it was each day – and we were anxious to get into our tent, take off our hiking boots and relax before our afternoon snack. On that particular day, however, our tent was on uneven ground; and when Pam and I went to lay down, we had to fight to keep from sliding toward the lower end of the tent. Realizing there was no way we could comfortably lie in the tent without ending up in a collective heap, we asked Haruni if it would be possible for the porters to move our tent so it would be more comfortable to sleep that night. We apologized for being an inconvenience, but Haruni merely laughed and said, "No problem, I had to have them move my tent as well." In a matter of minutes our tent was moved by two of the porters, and they waited to make sure it was done to our satisfaction. We nodded yes and replied, "Asante sana." They smiled back at us in a way that let us know they were happy to have served us well. We also received the same type of care when the zipper on the toilet tent got stuck a few times.

We were also struck by our team's care for us when Haruni described what would happen on the night of our summit attempt. He explained that we would leave around midnight, go up to the summit and return later in the day, arriving back at our same camp. After a short rest we would gather our belongings and move further down the mountain. Because we were leaving and then returning to the same site for the first time, camp would not need to be broken until we returned from the summit. Haruni mentioned that one of the porters would sleep in our tent after we left to make sure our belongings were safe. With the exception of the guides and guests, everyone (including the numerous other outfitters) would stay in camp while the hikers went up the mountain; therefore, our belongings might be at risk if left unattended. Still more attention to detail by our team!

We never actually saw our camp being broken down each day because we left each morning as tear-down was just getting started. I would have loved to see their teamwork as they went through this daily process. I can imagine how efficient they were because they passed us on the mountain only 60 to 90 minutes after we left. Each day the entire camp is broken down into "increments" of no more than 32 lbs. per porter, and then those "increments" were thrown onto the backs, heads and shoulders of our team. Each morning we waved and said goodbye to our team as we walked away, only to see them a short while later. We would hear a cheerful "Mama" and "Dadee" and we would turn around and see our team coming up quickly behind us. In a matter of moments, we would be passed on the trail and they would slowly fade into the distance further up the mountain. We would then show up at our next camp to see it already set up and awaiting our arrival. It's hard to imagine that the best NFL team performance would rival what happened each day on the side of Kilimanjaro.

Who is Rich? Who is Poor?

As you may well imagine, the work our team performed each day was difficult. And yet, their smiling faces and laughter were constants. We drifted off to sleep each night listening to voices chattering and the laughter of our team. I'm sure there was plenty of ribbing, joking and inside jokes being told by a bunch of guys who worked together on a regular basis. Each person took on their role with a joyful attitude, whether it was the leader or the lowest ranking member of the team. What their "status" was didn't seem to matter to them; everyone got along well and they were happy with their contribution to the team. Amazingly, all of this was being done while most of them made only $40 to $50 per week. It made me wonder how different my life would be if I didn't care if I received credit for my work; rather, if I just basked in the satisfaction of knowing that I had supported the efforts of the team. I know that this is how I should feel and act, but it was different to see it played out successfully in front of me. I was amazed by the humble and giving nature of our team. "Rich" took on another meaning. Most Americans are definitely "rich" in terms of money when compared to those in Africa. But what I saw there revealed something quite different. I felt "poor" when I recognized how this team operated compared to many of the teams I have been a member of. I was reminded of the Harry S. Truman quote: "It is amazing what you can accomplish if you do not care who gets the credit."

☙

Truman's quote, and our experience on Kilimanjaro, caused me to think about how different many U.S. companies might be if they shared the same spirit and attitude of the Tanzanian people. How different would we be if we were all joyful in the work we performed? How different would we be if we were all more focused on getting the job done, rather than our contribution to the outcome?

Who Surrounds You?

A good start to surrounding yourself with a good team is to surround yourself with like-minded people. Many of us heard while growing up, "You are who you hang out with." I have learned that the people with whom you surround yourself either lift you up or bring you down; they motivate you or drain you; they support you or criticize you; they make you laugh or make you cry. If you surround yourself with great people, you will tend to become great. If you surround yourself with mediocre people, you will tend to become mediocre. If you surround yourself with unmotivated people...Well, you get the idea. It is also important to work with people of like character.

It was difficult to pick a touring company, because there were so many variables. Many of the companies were based in Africa and

89

some were based in America. Some companies use only their own employees and some outsource the work to local Tanzanian companies. Some were affiliated with organizations that protect the porters such as the Kilimanjaro Porters Assistance Project and others were not. We wanted to work with an outfitter based in Africa who employed local Tanzanians and had a record of treating their porters well. We also read that we should make sure that the tips intended for each team member were not kept by the lead guide. Kindoroko Tours checked off all of those boxes and was the best match for us. This was our one chance to climb Kilimanjaro and we needed a touring company that reflected our values.

Diversity Makes a More Talented and Productive Team

We must also celebrate our differences. We can't have a team that consists of only salespeople, because we would run really fast in one direction and have no idea if that was the proper path. We also can't have a team entirely made up of engineers because – while we might not make a mistake along the way – it might take us forever to get where we are going. To be successful, a team requires a group of individuals with diverse talents. An NFL team needs players who can block, run, throw, catch, kick, and tackle. In the same way, a successful team in business needs people with different skills and experiences. By assembling a team of people from different backgrounds and experiences, who also think differently about certain issues, a manager greatly increases his or her chances of success.

I have worked with many companies that have all of the appropriate "players" on their team, but they have the punter playing quarterback and the offensive tackle playing wide receiver. They don't have everyone in the "right seat on the bus." Having the right people for the right job is critical. Almost every position on your team requires a different skill set. Managers, salespeople, technical experts and customer support staff all have different skills. Some people can perform multiple functions, but most cannot do everything well.

Therefore, you must be able to identify who will perform best at what position. In sales, every moment a salesperson who is gifted at being a "hunter" (acquiring new customers) spends his time as a "farmer" (focused on existing accounts), the organization sacrifices productivity. The same goes for product management, operations, etc. A "hunter" and a product manager are two very different positions that require very different levels of expertise. While the professional salesperson can expertly negotiate and strategize how to pursue the account, the technical person has the ability to identify and solve the technical problem. When we asked Haruni and Ema what it took to become a guide, we learned that each guide started as a porter. Every guide must also speak very good English and show proficiency on each Kilimanjaro route. Haruni had been a porter and could still perform that role, but his talents were best used as a guide. Each of our porters was very good at their role, but they weren't ready to become a guide; and perhaps they would never be. Similarly, in sales it is important to avoid mixing the wrong skill sets.

The Handoff

Salespeople must also delegate the responsibilities that take them away from selling. There are very few people in each organization who are skilled at selling, so every moment a salesperson *isn't* selling is time lost that can't be recovered. As a salesperson you need to concentrate on selling and you need all available time to do this. You need to surround yourself with people who will make your job easier so you can focus on your unique ability and do what you do best.

Salespeople are very talented, but often think they can do it all. That can really stall the growth of the pipeline. I often think my most important role as a sales manager is to "clear the runway" by removing the obstacles that get in the way of my sales team's productivity. By "handing off" some of your day-to-day back-office tasks, you will have more time to focus on generating revenue. Take a look at your weekly tasks and try to separate those you are comfortable with (and good at) from those that take too much time because you don't have the skills you need. Delegate those tasks. As Ronald Reagan said, "Surround yourself with the best people you can find, delegate authority, and don't interfere as long as the policy you've decided upon is being carried out."

Embracing what makes each of us different is an important first step in assembling the right team. You don't have to be a manager to assemble a team, but you *do* need to understand your strengths and weaknesses and find the appropriate people to support your work. There were many aspects of our trek that we didn't need help with, but navigating Kilimanjaro was definitely where we needed help. We would have had the endurance to make it to the summit, but not the knowledge on how to do so. We had the strength to carry our daypacks, but not the strength to carry our daypacks, duffel bags, tents, food, water, etc. We needed to surround ourselves with the right team and we wanted that team to reflect our values and character. We were blessed to find the perfect team of people to lead us and support us. If you aren't experiencing that on your team, identify the skill sets needed and go out and find the right people. They *are* out there.

CHAPTER 14

ILLUMINATE YOUR WAY

On Friday, we arrived at Barafu Camp, elevation 15,331 feet. It had taken five full days to reach this point and we had hiked 40 km (21 miles). Although we had been near this altitude before — when we were at Lava Tower in the middle of Day 3 — we hadn't stayed at this elevation for any extended period. This was for two reasons: 1) We were making our way around the south face of the mountain to where we would finally make our summit ascent; and 2) we were "hiking high and sleeping low" in order to acclimate ourselves to the higher — and potentially dangerous — altitude. As part of this acclimatization process, over the previous three days, we had climbed 3,000 to 4,000 feet every morning and then descended again to near our original altitude in the afternoon. While doing this, we made our way from west to east across the southern slopes of Kili to arrive at Barafu Camp, the staging ground for tomorrow's summit attempt. We hoped that this form of up-and-down acclimatization had prepared us for what lay ahead.

To that point, it had certainly been a difficult trip, but it appeared that the toughest part of the trek was yet to come. The words from the couple we met at breakfast on Monday morning still rang in our ears. We had seen them loading their luggage into a Land Cruiser. Their duffel bags looked similar to the style we were taking up Kili, so we asked them if they had just climbed the mountain. They said they had just returned the day before. We then asked them about their trek. They said it was "good." We, of course, wanted more information, so we asked them if it was difficult. They glanced at one another and the man said, simply, "The summit night was tough." It appeared that would be all the information we would get from them. They were 10 to 15 years younger than Pam and me, but at that point, "*tough*" didn't overly concern us. But now, just ahead of summit night – the only part of the climb they had commented on – that single word, tough, resonated in our heads. We suspected that the toughest part of our journey was indeed yet to come.

Early to Bed, Very Early to Rise

Our normal routine was moved up an hour or so after we arrived at Barafu Camp: tea and popcorn was early, dinner was early, our briefing with Haruni and Ema was early, and we were told to try to go to sleep at 7:00 p.m. Haruni told us that Iddi would wake us around 11:30 p.m.; we would then have tea and popcorn and set off up the mountain soon after. We were also told that all of the other gear we had purchased would now be needed. We were warned by Haruni that the hike to the summit would be tough – there was that *word* again! – and that we would likely get a bad headache, experience some light-headedness, feel nauseated, and probably throw up. (I was beginning to wonder why I paid hard-earned money for the privilege of feeling this way!)

I first realized the effect of the altitude when I rolled over from my back to my stomach inside my sleeping bag. After trying to straighten out my sleeping bag, I started to put my head on my pillow. That small amount of activity made it very hard to breathe. We were at just over 15,000 feet and the impact of the lack of oxygen even while we rested was severe; we couldn't imagine what tomorrow would be like when we were exerting ourselves. Pam told me she understood how I felt, because she had just walked back 10 steps from the "toilet tent" and had to sit down to catch her breath before zipping up the tent. We knew we were in for a short night of sleep, but we were only able to sleep for one hour, due to going to bed early, the high elevation and being anxious about the hike ahead. When we finally did fall asleep, it felt like mere minutes until we heard Iddi say softly, "Mama," "Dadee." It was time to get up.

Bundled, But Still So Very Cold

We bundled up in all the clothes we purchased for this one occasion. I wore long underwear, 2 pair of pants, 3 shirts, a down jacket and an outer shell, a pair of gloves with liners, a head lamp, hat and a buff to go around my neck. It was hard to imagine that four days earlier we were hiking in shorts and short-sleeved technical shirts. Luckily, we didn't have to bring our backpacks with us, but I did have to keep our camera under all the layers of my clothing because of the even colder weather to come. We stood outside our tent for a few minutes waiting for Haruni and Ema. Pam said she was miserable. She told me she was so hot with all the extra clothes on and threatened to go back to the tent and remove some of her clothes before we started hiking. Fortunately, she did not and the reason for this was quite evident as we moved out onto the exposed trail and away from Barafu Camp. Words cannot describe how bone-chilling cold it was; I asked Pam if she was unhappy that she didn't leave some of her clothes behind. She quickly admitted that she wanted to keep everything on she had brought!

We were one of the last groups to leave Barafu Camp, and as we looked up the mountain trail we could see small lighted dots zigzagging up the mountain. The lighted dots we saw were from the head lamps worn by each climber. We had put them on before while in our tent each night to help us see, but this was the first time we would use them for hiking. It was 12:30 a.m., with nearly a full moon, but the head lamps were needed to make sure we were stepping in safe places.

Two Steps Forward, One Step Back

The terrain was unlike anything I had ever seen. I can't imagine the moon's surface being too different. There were long stretches of boulders 2-3 feet in circumference, often stacked on top of one another. When there weren't boulders, there was scree one foot deep. Walking through scree is exhausting; it is the perfect example of two steps forward and one step back. We were climbing at such a severe incline that we each needed to push off on our back foot in order to propel ourselves forward. The foot-deep scree made that push forward nearly impossible. The large boulders were even worse. At altitude, it took so much effort to get on top of each boulder and that effort is what affected Pam the most. We would often have to stop every 20-30 yards to catch our breath. The lack of oxygen, coupled with the physical effort, made it very difficult to breathe. Our experience was not unique. We constantly passed groups sitting down on boulders trying to catch their breath, only to see them 15 minutes later pass us as we were sitting down. We even saw our young "rabbit" friends a few times. They kept moving along so fast and we doubted that they could continue to sustain that effort. It didn't take long for us to go by them, never to be seen again. (Go "turtles"!)

Even though we had already climbed 4,000 feet on two of the previous days, this night climb was so much harder. The terrain made it very difficult, but the severity of the slope was a bigger obstacle. It was so steep that we had to "switchback" every 5 to 8 feet. Switchbacks are the equivalent of zigzagging up the mountain, so each step is less severe. The other challenge was the weather. We learned that the temperature was 2 degrees Fahrenheit, with 45 mph wind gusts. Even with all of the layers of clothing we had on, we were freezing!

Solitude

The night-into-morning summoned unexpected solitude. We were surrounded by other hikers, yet there was only one narrow trail up the mountain, so everyone was in single file formation. The wind also made it difficult to communicate, so you were often left to your own thoughts. It reminded me a lot of the end of a marathon, where it felt like you were running on empty. I typically had enough energy to finish, yet I battled the inner demons that told me I couldn't make it, it was just too tough. I also worried about Pam, because she wasn't feeling well. I kept thinking about that couple at Bristol Colleges that would only tell us the summit night was "tough." They probably used that single word, "tough," because the truth might have been more than we could handle. As Colonel Jessup said in the movie *A Few Good Men*, "You can't handle the truth!" Maybe we couldn't have handled the truth in the beginning, but now we had no choice but to face it head on: this part of the climb was indeed TOUGH.

CR

Just as our headlamps showed us where we could step with confidence, in sales, leading indicators can reveal the probable success of your current path. Without leading indicators, you are taking your next step and hoping that you land on solid footing. "Hope" is a wonderful thing, but not when you use it as a sales strategy. Businesses need to know "how it's going" well before the final results are recorded. The way to do that is to define and start measuring leading indicators.

What *is* a Leading Indicator?

Leading indicators are predictive measurements. While hiking, not drinking often enough is a leading indicator for feeling weak, due to dehydration. The financial reports you review at the end of the month, quarter or year are *lagging* indicators. No matter when you receive them – a day, 10 days, 30 days or even 10 minutes after the time frame of that period – they are still lagging indicators, reporting what has already happened.

You don't want to discover crucial failing issues too late. Leading indicators are the "warning lights" that something isn't working or something has gone wrong. These warning lights allow you the opportunity to intervene before it is too late. Today's fast-paced environment necessitates that your business have leading indicators to help you take corrective measures quickly. These indicators can be positive or negative, but either way, they signal an action to take. Wouldn't you rather be proactive than reactive? The nature of a leading indicator helps you to be proactive, to make changes ahead of the curve. After the fact, of course, is too late. Most metrics are an autopsy; they are lagging indicators about which absolutely nothing whatsoever may be done to change the result. A leading indicator can be as simple as the leads that you generate. If you have quantified the number of leads you are getting, then these can be a good predictor of your future sales conversions. You must find your own unique leading indicators that predict your future outcomes. On Kilimanjaro, our water intake, our food consumption, taking breaks when we were tired and the twice daily oximeter testing were all leading indicators of our probability of success.

No salesperson or sales manager should ever be surprised that they missed their quota or target numbers. Nor should they be surprised by their manager's response to their performance. Or by being put on a performance improvement plan, or required to take other actions to improve their results. Each of us should have advance notice that we need to improve. Knowing and communicating what those leading indicators are will do that for you. On the third day of our trip, Pam and I failed to drink enough water and it affected how we felt in the afternoon. We weren't surprised by how we felt; it was our fault, we didn't take enough hydration breaks. It was a lesson we didn't have to repeat. We got away with it that day, but we might not be able to recover in the future. So it is in sales; "warning lights" help salespeople measure themselves against their leading indicators before it is too late. Consider looking at your scheduled appointments, face-to-face sales calls, opportunities in your pipeline and the movement of opportunities from one sales cycle stage to the next. Great salespeople hold themselves accountable, but good leaders can help their team by holding their salespeople accountable for results. The best leaders know it is unfair to hold people accountable for poor sales without first holding them accountable for producing the results captured by leading indicators.

Measuring to Predict the Outcomes You Want

When looking at leading indicators, sales *metrics* are often confused with sales *activities*. Sales managers should focus their sales teams on sales activities and measure those leading indicators. Sales metrics are important, but, again, they are lagging indicators of success. The only types of metrics sales teams can affect are the tactical sales activities. Unfortunately, most sales teams only focus on and measure sales metrics, so it's challenging to diagnose why salespeople miss quota. If we don't know what should have occurred in order to give the salesperson the best chance to succeed, we won't know what didn't happen that should have. We are evaluating the game after the final score has been posted. Being dehydrated and putting the rest of the day's hike at risk is too late. Knowing that I need to take a break and drink water every 30 minutes allows me to put myself in the best position to succeed; it also allows me to know what didn't go well if I find myself dehydrated.

The key for your business is to discover what measurements you need to be taking in order to predict the outcomes you want. These are your leading indicators and they allow you to make decisions before the lagging indicators reveal what has truly happened. Companies with sales professionals use KPIs (Key Performance Indicators) to make better decisions, relying on something more specific than an educated guess to measure long-term success. If you were playing a baseball game, wouldn't you want to know in the 3rd inning if you were on track to lose the game? Wouldn't you want to know before the game was over that you should do something different? In the same way you can look back on successful baseball games and learn why you won, you can look back on how you were able to acquire new clients. Find out why you "won" those new clients and focus on and evaluate those criteria in the future.

Ask yourself these questions:

- Which indicators do you spend more time with – leading indicators or lagging indicators?
- Do most of the reports you receive and use contain leading indicators or lagging indicators?
- What are the most important leading indicators you measure and monitor?
- How do you use leading indicators to help improve your own performance or your team's performance?

Reaching your quota is a lot like reaching the summit of Kilimanjaro; it doesn't have to be a surprise – there are plenty of mile markers along the way to show you whether you are on the right path. Selling is "tough" enough; don't make it more difficult than it already is.

CHAPTER 15

"NO" IS THE SECOND
BEST ANSWER

On each of the first five days of our trip, we hiked in the morning for 4 to 5 hours and then rested while we ate lunch. On Summit Day, we had hiked for over 5 hours and lunch was still a long way away. We were operating on one hour of sleep and we were exhausted. We didn't know how much longer it would take us to get to the summit, but we knew it wouldn't be easy. Stella Point sat at 18,800 feet and it was about an hour's hike from there to the summit. But how far were we from Stella Point? We looked up at the steep climb ahead and there was nothing to indicate how close we were to the top. There had been many hikers ahead of us due to their early start, but we hadn't seen anyone coming back down after having reached the summit. Where were they? Where were we? It was 5:40 a.m., still dark, and we weren't yet at Stella Point.

What we did know was that Pam was beginning to struggle.

Going into the climb, she had been in great shape; and she had been more than up to the challenge day after day as we climbed higher into the sky. But I knew that she couldn't control being light-headed, nauseous and having a headache – all among the high altitude-related symptoms that Haruni had warned us about. Throughout this entire trip we didn't experience any muscle soreness, so we knew we were in good shape. What we worried about is what we couldn't control. I had been fortunate to get through food poisoning the first day, but would we be lucky enough to avoid all the consequences of high altitude sickness that cause 57% of people to fail to make it to the top? I was really tired, but I felt good enough to make it. I wasn't sure how badly Pam was hurting. Our rest breaks were occurring more often, and they were lasting longer. She was quiet, withdrawn. I didn't know how long – or even if – she could continue.

Reaching Stella

Sunrise occurred at 6:27 a.m., and although we were not at the summit to see the sun come up, the view was still spectacular. We stopped for a moment to take it in. First, the horizon began to glow in a beautiful pink-orange hue and from our vantage point the edge of the earth became clearly defined. From nearly 18,871 feet we could see the curvature of the earth at the far ends of the horizon. One word: Breathtaking. Literally. The rising sun also brought some much needed warmth. Haruni informed us that the wind normally dies down after sunrise – good news! But what I really wanted to know was: where is Stella Point? Shouldn't we be getting close? Sunlight also brought negative signs. We saw the exhaustion in the faces of our fellow hikers on the trail and we prayed that we didn't look that bad (even though I knew we probably did). We also discovered others were sick, because we passed the evidence in places where they had revisited their last meal. And finally, we began to see the first few people coming down the mountain. It should have been encouraging, yet it seemed somewhat depressing to know that they were experiencing the joy of going downhill while we still struggled going uphill. They also seemed to look a whole lot better than we felt.

We reached Stella Point at 7:30 a.m., and, oh, what a welcome sight it was to see the sign that we had viewed so often online. It read *"Congratulations! You are now at Stella Point. Alt. 5739M A.M.S.L. Tanzania."* (I resisted the urge to scream "Stelllllaahhh!")

Stella Point was on rather flat ground; and we immediately found a place to sit. We had made it this far, but we knew we still had an hour to go. Haruni pointed up and off to the right to show us where Uhuru Peak was; it was the first time we could actually see the top. I felt a renewed sense of encouragement, but it soon dissipated as I considered how Pam felt. I could tell she was hurting, and it reminded me of our pact: *If one of us couldn't go on, the other would.* It would be hard for me to make it the rest of the way, but I knew I would make it. Still, I didn't want to stand atop the summit without her. We had been married for 27 years at that point, yet I wasn't sure how to ask her if she could continue. Should I be supportive and let her know that I would support either decision, or was this the time I should refuse to take "no" for an answer? If she told me to go on without her, was I supposed to push her to find some hidden strength she didn't know she had, or accept her answer empathetically?

What made this uncertainty worse was that Haruni and Ema began pacing. Throughout our climb they had been supportive and encouraging, exuding confidence and instilling in us a sense of inevitable achievement. But now Haruni and Ema looked worried. "Do not sit long, Mama," Ema said. "We have to keep going." I asked for a few moments, even though they had warned us if we didn't begin again soon it could be quite dangerous. They both nodded, but I could see in their body language they were worried. Their jobs were to get us to the top of the mountain, something they had done many times with others. I knew that they would see our failure as their failure, too.

Summoning the Will to Continue On

Pam looked up. She managed a smile. But as I left her to regain her strength and gather her thoughts, I was flooded with my own. I thought back to how it all started, with a wild idea jotted down while sitting at a café in Australia, and to all the training and preparation since. I remembered scaling the toughest Smoky Mountain trails, pushing our bodies to their limits (or so I had thought). I recalled the hours of hiking through a driving downpour, slipping and sliding on the trails at Turkey Run. I thought back to all the research and planning, to the weeks of assembling essential supplies and equipment. I thought about the five days so far on this mountainside: hiking for miles, at times on seemingly endless winding switchback trails, scaling massive boulders and trudging through the quicksand-like scree where we measured progress in inches. I replayed all of it in my head, including how it was me that almost didn't make it past the first day. And now here we were, so close to the top of the tallest mountain in Africa.

I knelt beside Pam. "You ready to go?" I asked, not at all certain whether she would join me in our attempt to reach the summit. Pam cleared her throat before taking my hand in hers. "I didn't come this far to give up now," she said firmly. I smiled and squeezed my wife's hand. I knew she was tough, but I learned that day how tough she really was. If she had said "no," that would have been okay. We needed to decide either way for our safety, but what I really wanted to hear – what I was *relieved* to hear – was a "yes." We took a couple of pictures of the Stella Point sign, but none of the two of us in front of that sign. THE sign and THE photo stood an hour ahead at Uhuru Peak!

"You Can Make It"

We were told the remaining climb wouldn't be as bad as the last seven hours. That was music to our ears! Pam continued to get sicker, however, stopping a few times because she felt like she might vomit. (She had the kind of nausea where you want to vomit because you think you will feel better, but she still couldn't quite bring herself to "enjoy" that experience.) So we continued on for another hour passing people headed down, most of them telling us "you can make it!" They smiled and were very encouraging. It took about an hour to reach Uhuru Peak; and there it was: the big green and yellow sign we had longed to see — THE photo opportunity. It was 8:40 a.m., more than eight hours since we had trudged out of Barafu Camp.

I looked at Pam and said "we made it, can you believe it?" Her tears caused me to cry. But we were not alone at the summit, as other groups had reached the top, too. As we spoke with others while waiting our turn to take pictures in front of the sign, we learned they were experiencing the same feelings as us: a euphoria so profound it was hard to put into words.

We could, however, find the words, "Thank you!" We hugged Haruni and Ema and thanked them again and again for their servant leadership and persistent care. We knew we couldn't have made it without them. After 15 minutes it was finally our turn for pictures. We had not only dreamed of this moment; we had planned for it, too. So we took photo after photo, making sure we captured every image we had planned.

And then, after less than a half hour on top of the world, it was time to come back down to earth and begin our descent. As we stepped away from the sign, I looked across the seemingly endless sky, and then I looked into my wife's eyes.

We had conquered Kilimanjaro! We had done it together.

CR

I have learned, over a 30-year career in sales, that the second best answer a prospect can give you is "no." At first, I thought I only wanted to hear "yes," because sales is a career where getting the answer "yes" is the demonstrative income making answer. If you are in commission-driven sales, you need "yes" in order to earn, so how could the idea of "no" be the second best answer? The basic premise is that the answer "no" is as final as "yes" is; it allows a salesperson to know where to spend time. Because time is one of the few commodities a salesperson has, it is imperative that it be spent in the most productive ways.

"No" allows a salesperson to move on and be given a new opportunity to hear "yes." Entirely too much time is spent chasing unlikely "yes's" and not moving on to greener pastures that afford income-making opportunities. The goal is not to minimize the importance of being professionally persistent, nor to ignore the art of relationship building. Time spent on both of these skills is well worth the investment IF the return justifies the time spent and we believe that a "yes" is possible.

Avoiding "Maybeland"

What you want to do is stay out of "maybeland." Maybeland is the worst place to be in the sales process. "Yes" is the best answer and "no" is the second-best answer. What can drive salespeople crazy is either no response or some sort of delay from the person they are trying to reach. This could be because 1) the prospect may not truly understand how you can assist them, or 2) they are not a qualified prospect, or 3) they are busy and have other priorities, or 4) they are just trying to be nice and don't want to let you down by actually saying "no." The problem is we often don't know the real reason and we don't know whether we should move on. At nearly 19,000 feet, Haruni and Ema knew that "maybe" could cause us to be very sick. "Yes" was the best answer and would take us to the summit, but "no" was the second best answer because we would go down the mountain where the decreasing altitude would help us feel better. Staying at "Stella Point" and not making a decision was not an acceptable answer.

It is also important to understand that "no" is not a bad word. "No" brings clarity. Think about the game 20 Questions. When we ask questions like "Is it bigger than a breadbox?" or "Is it a person, place or thing?," we don't view the response "no" as being negative; quite to the contrary, we are happy that we are a step closer to the answer. A "no" in sales should be viewed the same way. We have been taught since childhood to fear it. Tom Hopkins explains in *How to Master the Art of Selling,* "We get it pounded into us that no is rejection – and rejection is painful. No is bad." But rejection is part of life. If something is worth doing, you are going to face obstacles. Hearing "no" from others should be manageable and can be positive. Every "no" you receive is valuable input. Listen to the feedback, understand the fears and doubts you are hearing, and learn from the experience. That way, the next time you make a presentation or proposal, you can adapt your message and get even better.

Turning "No" Into a "Yes"

Hearing "no" also helps you to discover the real concern. With "no," you have something to work with. "No" enables you to search for alternatives. Remember, some prospects are not a good fit for what you are selling. The need may not be there, or the timing may not be right. Either way, the sooner you discover whether you have a qualified prospect or not, the better. The main thing to realize is that "no" isn't necessarily a conversation ender. In fact, it can be used as a very effective conversation *driver* in the sales process. Ask the prospect "What led you to that decision?" or "Why do you say that?" or "Really. I'm a bit surprised. Tell me more?" If all else fails, ask, "Why?" If Pam had said "no" to my question, it would have allowed me to understand why she didn't think she could go on. She might have said "no" because she couldn't walk at the same pace we had earlier. Knowing that was her true concern would have allowed us to make a decision to walk at a slower pace and turn that "no" into a "yes."

We all find ourselves at times in "maybeland." We may have failed to ask the necessary questions and landed in a place where we don't know what the prospect wants to do next. Time is slipping away and we don't know how to get to a "yes" or a "no." The key is to make it easy for someone to tell you "no." Sounds counterintuitive, right? Remember, we want "yes" first, "no" second and "maybe" last. We have to put ourselves in our prospects' shoes. It is hard to tell you "no," so a prospect often avoids telling you, which is worse than knowing the true answer. Let them know that "no" is an acceptable answer, so they are more likely to tell us what they already know is the answer. Send them an email that lets them know that this is the last time you will reach out to them, but still leave the door open to future conversations. You will find this approach typically gets a response – it is just as likely to be a "yes" or a "no," but as we have learned, either one is okay. We just needed to get them to answer us and indicate their preference.

If you have viewed the word "no" as a bad word, it is time to retrain your brain. Instead, view "no" as a tool that gets you closer to "yes." Whether it is moving on to a new client more quickly or finding the real concern and overcoming it, "no" saves you time. Continue to hope for a "yes" as I did from Pam at Stella Point, but if you hear "no," just know that now you have something to work with and your real task can begin.

CHAPTER 16

DOWNHILL IS NOT ALWAYS EASIER THAN UPHILL

Although it had been 8 ½ long hours since we had set out from Barafu camp, Pam and I actually had a little hop in our steps. Following all the photographs, "high fives" and hugs, we began to make our way back down to Stella Point, which we assumed would be a fairly easy walk. After 5 ½ days we were finally going down! Our route up the mountain had been both up and down, but now there was no more "up," there was only "down." We were now ready to take on the last day and a half of our trek.

We began retracing our steps back to Barafu Camp, but this time we could see where we were going. Once we arrived at camp, we would rest for about an hour and get something to eat, then pack up our duffel bags, pick up our backpacks and continue on down the mountain. We were looking forward to this part of the journey, thinking it would be much easier. With the exception of Haruni and Ema who summited with us, the remainder of our crew stayed back at Barafu Camp awaiting our return. After descending only about 30 minutes, we passed Stella Point (and again, I resisted the urge to cry out "Stellllaaaahh!"). Now we were really moving!

Surfing!

As we descended, we passed a few groups still making their way to the summit, and we gave them the same encouragement that we had received. "You're almost there!" We realized we must have had the same pained look on our faces a short while ago as they did. We knew they would make it, and we smiled and told them so. We paused briefly at the Stella Point sign to once again take in the view before moving on. We were now looking down at the path we had taken in the dark just two hours ago — and it was *steep*. Did we really come up THAT? And suddenly our trek downward became more treacherous. It would be a lot harder to step down a few feet than it had been to step up. Not as exhausting, perhaps, but certainly more precarious. We started downward and descended this steep section of Kilimanjaro for about 30 more minutes. With each step we became less and less excited about "down."

We then moved past the large boulders and encountered the quicksand-like scree that had been our evil nemesis on the ascent. In the bright sunlight, we now realized how deep the scree was and how far it extended down the mountain. How on earth did we climb up through that stuff?!? Just a couple of hours earlier we had gotten a sense of what it was like when our head lamps shone on the ground, but at that time we had been climbing single file and could only see a few feet ahead. Now, looking down, all we could see below us was a mountain layered in scree.

Luckily, we were able to take a more direct (shorter) path down the mountain, and except for a few places, didn't have to take the switchbacks. The direct path presented us with a new experience: *scree surfing!* The first few minutes of "surfing" down the mountain were fun, but the fun faded rather quickly. It was like walking down stairs, but it felt like you were skipping a step — your foot landed well below where you took the step from. We led with the heel of our boot. Once we landed, we would slide for a foot or two, then stop from the buildup of scree. Common sense told us that the scree would eventually stop us, but at times we felt like we were on the verge of being out of control. I was reminded of the scene from the movie *Stripes,* where John Candy's character was out of control running pell-mell through the obstacle course. He was moving so fast that he veered off the course. If that happened to us, "off the course" would be off the mountain.

At Long Last, Pain

Ema was leading our descent and he seemed to be waiting on us every 10 minutes or so. His long legs and lanky frame were well-suited for this type of descent. If I were a "beanpole" and 25 years old, I might have been better at it, too! All in all, it took us 4 hours to get back to Barafu Camp, and we arrived to the applause of our support team. They were all lined up at the edge of camp, anticipating our arrival. They cheered, hugged us, and even dusted off our gaiters. We were exhausted, but it felt so good to celebrate. We were only at the summit for a short time before we had to turn around and start back down the mountain, so it felt like the first time we could actually pause and just take it in. We were also really hungry! It had been over 13 hours since we had enjoyed tea and popcorn at 11:30 p.m. the previous night. We had a brief lunch and were told we could sleep for an hour before packing up our duffel bags and continuing down the mountain. Pam and I commented that we couldn't believe we weren't done for the day. Haruni said we wouldn't go through any more scree, so we were encouraged to hear that. After lunch, Pam immediately fell asleep for an hour, but I couldn't sleep. My wife has always been able to take naps, but I rarely am able to do so. Oh, how I wished I could have slept, if even for those few minutes.

At about 2:00 p.m., we set out on the extremely direct Mweka Route toward Mweka Camp, a descent from 15,331 feet to 10,065 feet. Our route was a series of "steps" that consisted of boulders surrounded by hard-packed soil. It resembled a staircase, where you would take one or two steps on each stair step before stepping down.

Once again, each step down was the equivalent of skipping a step — much like the scree from earlier in the day. This severe decline continued for 4 or 5 hours. We had gone the entire trek without pain of any kind, and now my knees were screaming! I began to step down on my left foot to minimize the pain in my right knee. As bad as it was, I don't know how we could have done it without trekking poles. Once again, Ema didn't seem to have any problems. Haruni used his trekking poles, but Ema literally skipped down the trail. (Ah, to be young again!)

Looking Up

It had been a very long day and we kept hoping to hear voices from people already at camp. It felt like a *sound mirage*, because I was certain that I heard voices a few times. It is also possible that I was getting a little looney at that point (Pam would tell you that didn't just start on this trek!) As the afternoon shadows lengthened, I took a few moments during one of our breaks to look around me. We were once again in the Montane Forest, in the midst of green again after days without it. And then I told Pam to look up. She wondered what I was talking about. I said, "The clouds." She smiled and nodded, recognizing, as I had, that it was the first time in days we could look UP to see the clouds.

Shortly after this break we were told it wouldn't be long before we would arrive at Mweka Camp; and soon two of our porters appeared, nimbly making their way up the path toward us. That was a good sign! They offered to take our backpacks and we gladly handed them over. We arrived at Mweka Camp a little more than 4 hours after leaving Barafu Camp. Mweka Camp was surreal: lush and green with dirt nearly black as coal, and the air was cool and damp; it even seemed "heavy." Higher oxygen levels! Haruni and Ema said tomorrow would be a much easier, 3 to 4 hour hike. We still had about 4,000 feet of decline, but for this moment, I was going to take them at their word. "Easier" sounded good to me!

Our day was now complete. All told, it had consisted of 17 hours of hiking on less than one hour of sleep. We had gone up 4,010 feet and down 9,276 feet. That couple at Bristol Cottages we had spoken with was right. This day had indeed been "tough!"

CR

Pam and I thought the downhill portion of our trek would be much easier than the uphill portion. It was faster and we were going downhill, so that would make sense, right? However, because we thought the worst part was behind us, we weren't prepared for the challenge that awaited us. This is similar to what it can be like after reaching your sales quota or landing that one large deal – the toughest work may still lie ahead. You might have worked really hard landing and supporting that big sale, only to realize that you don't have much left in the pipeline for next year. It is like a roller coaster ride. Imagine going up and down hills at 100 miles per hour one moment, only to come to a screeching halt the next. Anyone with a long career in sales has experienced the roller coaster ride where you are crushing your revenue targets one quarter or year, only to fall completely on your face the next. By experiencing that, you have gone through boom and bust revenue production.

Staying Off the Roller Coaster

Your goal should be to have your performance follow a smooth, upward path that yields a perpetual sales boom. And that boom doesn't have to be – and shouldn't be – followed by a bust on the other side. The joy we felt when making it to the summit was quickly followed by the frustration of a really difficult descent. Despite our rigorous training for the uphill climb, we weren't ready for the downhill. We were able to get away with not being prepared this one time, and in sales you can get away with not performing the right activities for a while. You might hit your annual revenue targets for a while, but even if you do, the side effects of this roller coaster ride will reveal themselves eventually. You need to hold yourself

113

accountable to metrics that drive revenue on a daily basis. If you are a sales manager, your responsibilities are to hold your team accountable. Too much emphasis in only one area will cause your team to lose sight of its ultimate goal: a smooth, upward path of increasing sales.

One way to avoid the roller coaster sales ride is to continue prospecting even when you are busy. Finding the time to prospect while you are selling or managing projects can be tough, but waiting to prospect until you are not busy is too late. While you are working on projects, you must set aside time to find, develop and cultivate existing or new relationships that will produce future work. We often celebrate a full pipeline, but dwelling in that period of celebration can often lead to an empty cupboard. When do salespeople concentrate most on prospecting? When they don't have enough sales opportunities in the works. The moment they do, they cast prospecting aside for activities that are more enjoyable. It is only a matter of time before they are back at square one – with no new leads to pursue. If you want to avoid the classic "feast or famine" approach and you want your pipeline to be more consistent, your prospecting efforts need to be consistent and constant. Don't let success prevent you from future growth by tying up your time as you service your newly found customers.

Planning for Prospecting

Another key to finding consistency is to have a plan. Who are your target prospects? Where can you find them? How many will you contact each day or week? When will you contact them? Via what channels? When will you conduct your research? It is vitally important to create a written plan and adjust as needed to maximize your results. For most of us, if prospecting is not scheduled, it doesn't get done. The time for prospecting has to be treated as if it were an important meeting. None of us would ever think of being late for, or skipping, an important meeting. It may also help to schedule this time during the time of day when you are sharpest, at your peak performance. Prospecting is hard work and most of us don't enjoy the activity, so make sure you are at your best when you need to be. You must avoid listening to the lie we often tell ourselves: "There's no time." You do have the time; you just need to schedule it into your day. A prospecting process requires regular activity, no matter what else is going on in your business. When you get busy — because you will — don't stop prospecting. Stay the course. Salespeople who stop prospecting ride the roller coaster of income: one month, great; the next, nothing. The ups and downs of income are caused by the inconsistency of their prospecting. Resolve today to keep up the momentum of prospecting.

We should still take time to celebrate our victories and revel in our accomplishments. Take time to reflect on your outstanding sales year or acquiring that large customer, in the same way Pam and I took some time at Uhuru Peak to absorb what we had just accomplished. But in order to be prepared for what lies ahead, don't invest all your energies into only one account or one year. Sales is not a water faucet where you can just turn on the leads, opportunities or sales immediately; they have to be nurtured every day. What's more, spending part of each week working on growing revenue via existing clients, in addition to prospecting for future clients, will enable you to sustain sales excellence year after year. You don't have to experience the highs of reaching your sales summit one year, only to be disappointed by your rapid descent the following year.

CHAPTER 17

ADJUST YOUR STYLE

The segment of our journey from the summit to our return to Barafu camp brings to mind one of the most poignant events of our week on Kilimanjaro. Let me elaborate. Before we had left Barafu Camp for our final push to the summit, Haruni told us that we would take only one backpack to the summit, which he would carry for us. The camelback in the backpack was filled with water, and we only took the essential items we would need for that night – the lightest load possible. From our research, we knew it was a very good possibility that our water tube (even though it was insulated) would freeze in the severe cold of summit night. It did. Fortunately, after the sun came up, the temperature on the mountain naturally increased enough for the line to clear and we were once again able to drink the water.

Summit night takes a lot out of a person, and your body requires additional water at altitude. Because Pam and I were both drinking from the same camelback, our water supply was exhausted well before we returned to Barafu Camp. As time passed while we descended the mountain, we began to feel the effects of dehydration.

Haruni softly said, "Mama, how are you feeling?" Pam said that, of

116

course, she was tired, but also that she was getting thirsty. Haruni then asked me how I was doing, and I replied the same. Haruni and Ema said we didn't have much longer to go, but we had heard that before; so I didn't know how much further it really would be before we reached Barafu Camp. My mouth was starting to feel rather dry, and that, along with the sun and increasing temperature, was beginning to take its toll.

Am I Hallucinating?

About an hour later, as I gazed down the mountain trail, I saw what appeared to be a human figure in the distance. This struck me as odd since we were now traveling the descent route. No one should have been coming UP this section of trail. Still, as we were in an area devoid of trees and bushes, I was able to watch this figure moving toward us from quite a long distance away. There wasn't much else to look at aside from rocks, dirt and boulders, so I began to fixate on that figure slowly moving toward us. As the figure drew closer I began to think it was Iddi – which didn't make any sense. At first, fearing I was hallucinating due to dehydration, I said nothing about this person approaching. But the closer he came, I finally mentioned the figure to Haruni and Ema. They didn't seem at all surprised. And soon enough, I could see that it was indeed Iddi making his way up the mountain. Iddi met us on a rock ledge and said in his soft-spoken voice, "Hello, Mama. Hello, Dadee." He (of course) wore a huge smile.

Iddi put down his backpack and began to take out a large bottle of fruit juice and a snack. We were never so happy to see anyone as we were to see Iddi at that moment! He handed Pam the bottle of juice, along with the snack, which she then shared with me. We had previously noticed during the week that most all the porters and guides had cell phones, and that they could in fact get a signal at certain points on Kilimanjaro. Evidently, during one of the few times that Ema fell back behind us, he called ahead and asked Iddi to come up the mountain to bring us something to eat and drink. Pam and I couldn't get over the fact that Iddi had hiked up the mountain – for 90 minutes – just to bring us something to eat and drink. While we could have made it to Barafu Camp without eating or drinking, we were beginning to struggle as we were deep into a very long day. Haruni and Ema knew we needed help, and Iddi was happy to accommodate. After giving us the juice and snack, Iddi pointed at our backpack that Haruni had carried up to the summit; Iddi said he would carry it down the trail to Barafu Camp. It was exactly what was needed, as we were about 90 minutes away from Barafu Camp and we still had 4-5 hours to go beyond that camp. Haruni and Ema were in tune with our needs at all times; they knew exactly what we needed at each moment. It was the same empathy and compassion that Haruni extended to me on Day One when I had suffered from food poisoning.

Giving Us What We Needed When We Needed It

Haruni and Ema adjusted their style of leadership and communication to fit what was needed at the time. They were assertive at Stella Point and Uhuru Peak when our health could have been at risk. They knew we needed to be pushed beyond our comfort zone and they encouraged us to keep moving when we didn't feel like we had much "left in the tank." They also encouraged us at many other points during our trip. But there was never a time when Haruni and Ema showed any doubt we would reach the summit. Their unwavering belief in us was contagious. We believed, in part, because *they* knew what it took to make it. And we believed them because they continuously told us we were doing great and they made us feel good about the progress we had made. They also encouraged us on summit night using more than just words. I remember Haruni leading us toward the summit, followed by Pam, me, and then Ema. During the toughest part of the climb, Haruni sang an African song. Pam commented during one of our breaks how much she appreciated hearing Haruni sing because it took her mind off how difficult the hike was. He repeated the verses to that song over and over because he knew it was what Pam needed at that time. Haruni and Ema were assertive, they were compassionate, and they were encouraging. They were all these things when they needed to be. They adjusted their communication styles to fit the situation.

These are the stories I remember most during our trek up and down Kilimanjaro. I remember the moments when I didn't think I could go much further, yet Haruni and Ema encouraged me. I remember when Pam and I were hurting and struggling and needed help – and each member of our team provided the assistance necessary. I think often of Iddi walking three hours round-trip to bring Pam and me the fruit juice and snack that was so badly needed. And I remember the joy on Iddi's face as he provided us with this help.

These wonderful friends of ours do not have MBAs, they do not have 30 years of corporate leadership experience, and they haven't been to sales training classes to learn how to deliver exactly what their customers need. Still, they delivered exactly what we (their customers) needed time and time again. They did so without being asked, and they did so without expecting anything in return. They did what they did because it was the right thing to do. They gave us what we needed - when we needed it most.

CR

Haruni and Ema adjusted their communication and leadership style to fit not only the situation, but to fit the person they were speaking with. They talked with me differently than they did with Pam. Although Pam and I enjoy many of the same activities, behaviorally we are totally different people. If you communicate with us in the same way at the same time, you will only connect with one of us. Sales is much the same. You need to adjust your behavioral style to fit your client's style of learning/comprehension. Too often, a salesperson uses his or her preferred style and runs the risk of not communicating adequately with clients. What if *your client's* learning/comprehension style is different than your preferred style? Can you recall a time when you were meeting with someone and they were overly excited, moving around quickly, talking fast, and your internal reaction was, "Whoa, slow down a bit!" Or maybe a time when you sat across from someone who behaved and communicated in exactly the opposite way? My guess is that you have experienced both ends of the spectrum and everything in between. How did these different styles make you feel? How did you react? Did they make you feel uncomfortable? Were the conversations you had difficult?

Mirroring the Customer

Life would be awfully boring if everyone was the same and there was no diversity or variety in communication styles. Nonetheless, it is that variety that makes communicating with others more difficult. Communicating with a prospect who shares my behavioral style is easy because I only need to think about how I would like someone to talk with me. For example, I like for people to get to the point and be succinct. An accountant or an attorney, however, might be the opposite – they might need and want as much data as they can get. As hard as it may be for me to adjust my communication style to fit those that need a lot of detail, I am thankful that my attorney and accountant are thorough and don't share my behavioral style.

As a salesperson, you will probably need to use all communication styles at different times, depending on the situation. The key is to remember that there is no single *best* style. The fact that you interact with different personality traits on a daily basis means that you must learn to quickly adapt and modify your message to them or it may get completely lost in translation. In sales terms, we call this adaptation, which involves "mirroring" the customer. What this means is that you must think of the space between you and your customer as a mirror, and then try to replicate what they do in terms of their communication style and body language.

To "mirror your customer" you must first define the customer's communication style preference. Their style of communication might be fast and direct or more pragmatic and slow. The most successful salespeople know how to communicate by matching – as closely as possible – the style of their customer. If they talk quickly, you will need to speed up your pace; if they sit on the edge of the chair and lean toward you when speaking, do the same. If they only want facts, make your message quick and to the point. Adjust your level of simplicity and complexity based on the cues you pick up from your customer or prospect. Listen closely and ask yourself how they seem to be talking and thinking. If they want it simple, keep it as simple and clear as possible. If your customer seems to want more complexity, go into greater depth and substance. Adjusting is a powerful way to build clarity, rapport and understanding.

Likability and Trust

It is often said that we "marry our opposites;" and while that may be true, customers buy from people like themselves – people whose styles they like and can relate to. In other words, people buy from people they like and trust. Typically, those whom they like and trust are the people who are most like them. So, if your *selling* style does not match the customer's *buying* style, it will be more challenging to form a bond of likability and trust. But if you are a salesperson who can adapt to the customer's style, you will have a better chance of getting the sale. The most effective way to gain the commitment and cooperation of others is to "get into their world" and adapt to their behavioral style. When you adapt your style to theirs, you build a bridge between the two of you, and they will respect your approach (because, after all, it's like their own). They will trust you more. They will think more highly of you.

I am amazed how often salespeople use one style – *their* style – to communicate with every customer. I have often observed a salesperson who loves to talk and isn't very detail-oriented move swiftly through a presentation with someone who needs detail. When customers who have a behavioral style that craves detail don't get the level of data needed, they get suspicious – they don't trust the salesperson. They think you move too fast and are reckless. And if you don't adjust your style, you will appeal to less than 25% of the population! Sales is hard enough without instantly eliminating 75% of your customer base. Imagine if, on Kilimanjaro, Haruni had pushed me too quickly when I had food poisoning on the first day; I would have instantly questioned whether I liked him and whether I wanted to follow him. But his form of communication in that situation was exactly what I wanted and needed; so my trust in him was immediate. He focused on what *I* needed, not what *he* needed or preferred. How different would sales be if we made that simple adjustment? Try it. You will love the results!

CHAPTER 18

TWO DAYS?

Ve awoke on Sunday morning finding it hard to believe it had been a week since we heard the congregation sing hymns at the church behind Bristol Cottages. We had started on Monday from the Machame Gate at an elevation of 5,718 feet, made it to Uhuru Peak at 19,341 feet yesterday and were now less than 5,000 feet from arriving at our destination – Mweka Gate (5,380 feet). We knew that today was a short hike of 3 hours and would be much easier on our knees.

The Tipping Point

We also knew that the "tipping ceremony" was to occur after breakfast. The "tipping ceremony" is Kindoroko Tours' routine where the hikers reward their team for a job well done. We were very pleased to learn of this ceremony, because in our pre-trip research we had read many accounts of how a lead guide might take all the tips and then not disseminate them to the team. We were anxious to thank each member of our team, not only in words, but financially. I had conducted some research before we left home to understand how much to tip each person. That process was easy when you didn't know the people. While we were prepared to tip what was appropriate, after spending a week with our team and benefitting from their hard work and support, we didn't feel good about how low the "suggested" amounts were. And now we had a problem — there was no ATM on the side of Kilimanjaro. So Pam and I decided that we were going to leave ourselves with only enough money for a small souvenir; the rest we would give to our team.

We asked Haruni at dinner the night before if he would write down the name of each team member and what their role on the team was. We had brought envelopes with us to put the tips in, and after receiving the list from Haruni, we wrote each team member's name on the outside of his envelope. The tipping ceremony began with the team singing and dancing to a few songs. Unfortunately, Dadee was encouraged to join in the dancing, and even more unfortunately, Pam had the video camera rolling. Envelopes were then passed out to each team member, and with words that were woefully inadequate, I expressed our gratitude for taking us on an adventure of a lifetime.

Mweka Gate

Following the tipping ceremony, the last part of the trip was indeed the easiest of the hike and we arrived at Mweka Gate around 11:00 a.m. Haruni and Ema were just as excited to have their first shower in a week as we were. When we arrived at Mweka Gate we saw porters bathing in a large trough, and I joked with Haruni about not being able to wait to get home to clean up. It was one of those moments when I wished I had kept my mouth shut; Haruni informed me that they were simply trying to get a quick wash in because they were going back up Kili only a few hours after coming down the mountain! While Haruni and I were checking in and signing the big book one last time, Ema was telling Pam how excited he was to get home and hold his baby girl (Dads all over the world are exactly the same!).

We picked up our gear, said our final goodbye to our team, and Pam, Haruni, Ema and I headed back to Bristol Cottages for lunch and to receive our finisher's certificates. We also looked forward to savoring the ice cold beer we had been craving the past week. It was suggested that we enjoy a Kilimanjaro Premium Lager. The local saying is, "If you can't climb it, drink it." We, of course, were now reveling in the fact that we *had* climbed it and were also about to drink it!

During lunch, our review of the events of the past week was non-stop, with much reflection and laughter. During our conversation, Pam asked Haruni and Ema if the team makes bets on how long, or how far, they believe each group will make it on the trip. Haruni just smiled, looked at Ema, and quietly held up two fingers. Pam caught on immediately, and asked if those two fingers meant two days. Ema grinned in his shy, slightly awkward way, shrugged and nodded "yes." Pam exclaimed, "You've got to be kidding me! Two days?!? Just two days?" Ema never really admitted that he had us pegged for heading back down the mountain after only two days; instead, he stated the reason we successfully made it to the top and back was because we listened, and that we did as we were told. Ema then recanted a story of a young woman who thought she knew better than the guides. He said she was very physically fit and well-trained, but wouldn't listen to their advice. Ema said she ate the wrong food, went way too fast, didn't drink enough water and basically did what she wanted to do, not what she should have done. She lasted a day and a half, and ultimately needed to be taken down the mountain by two porters on the team.

With Age Comes Wisdom

Pam and I reflected upon what Ema had said and realized he was right. We knew that Ema, Haruni and the others had been up and down the mountain hundreds of times, and this was our first and most likely only trip. We drank when they told us to drink, ate what was put in front of us, wore the clothing they recommended, and basically did what they said to do *when* they said to do it. If Haruni and Ema said, "Jump!," we said, "How high?" At 50 and 49, we are not what one would consider "spring chickens," and we in fact were among the oldest trekkers on the mountain that week. We laughed and told Ema and Haruni that becoming older brings the advantage of wisdom!

We also realized that there were countless examples of Pam and I doing exactly what our guides told us to do. We knew hydration was extremely important in order to avoid altitude sickness, and at Haruni and Ema's direction we drank a lot of water. We packed four liters of water daily for each of us. Three liters of water were carried in our camelbacks, along with an additional one liter bottle. The additional one liter bottle was filled with water boiled the night before at dinner time. Following dinner each evening Iddi brought Pam and me our bottle of boiled water. We took the boiled water to our tents and added two pills to the water: one pill was an iodine pill to get rid of impurities and the second pill – added 30 minutes later – was needed to remove the rather unpleasant iodine taste.

Nights on the side of Kilimanjaro tend to be quite chilly (an understatement), and we were instructed to put the bottle of hot water deep inside our sleeping bags to keep our feet warm – yet another example of our guides' wisdom and direction. However, Pam apparently is a better listener than I am, as during the first night I didn't put the hot water bottle in my sleeping bag. As you can imagine, I woke up in the middle of night with freezing feet! The next morning I learned that Pam's feet were toasty all night long. At that point, we were only at 10,000 feet, so I couldn't imagine not listening to our guides' advice in the nights that followed.

In the mornings, our camelbacks were filled and given to us after breakfast for the purification process. The beauty of the system was that when we started our journey after breakfast each morning, we were able to drink from the one liter bottle that had previously been hot the night before, but now was cold. When this cold bottle of water ran out, we switched to the water in our camelbacks which had been treated that morning and was now cool. I love it when a plan comes together! Could we have survived without following the system our guides taught us? Yes, but we wouldn't have had hot water to help keep us warm at night and we would've had to wait for our morning camelback water to purify and cool!

15 Pounds

Food consumption was a close second to water consumption. Haruni was always trying to get us to eat. Mind you, at altitude your appetite wanes and you really don't feel like eating very much; but Haruni was relentless. He would simply pick up our plates and heap more food on them, saying, "Mamaaa," or "Dadeee, you need to eat more!" So, we ate whatever Haruni told us to eat, and we were heartily congratulated after each meal on having a clean plate! Even so, it is amazing that we both lost approximately 15 pounds that week! I have been on a lot of vacations over the years and I don't think I've ever lost weight, let alone 15 pounds. Obviously, being on your feet for an entire day carrying a loaded backpack, takes a lot of energy. We would not have fared as well had we not eaten as much as we were told to.

When it came to what we were to wear each day, we wore exactly what Haruni told us to wear. We packed clothing appropriate for Fahrenheit temperatures ranging from the 80's to below zero. We knew what our itinerary said about expected weather conditions for each day, but we learned to trust what our guides said, not what a piece of paper stated. As an example, we needed to have our waterproof pants and jackets in our backpacks the first two days because we were beneath the clouds. Over the next 3+ days we didn't need that gear easily accessible in our backpacks because we were above the clouds and not subject to rain. We also didn't wear our gaiters the first day, but we were instructed to wear them each successive day. (Gaiters go over your boot tops, covering your leg below the knee, thereby keeping debris from entering your boots.) We had no idea how much of a climate change we were going to endure; and moving from a tropical climate to climates without foliage led to a great deal of dust, dirt and rock. On summit night, with temperatures hovering around zero and with winds gusting to 40 to 50 miles per hour, we were long past the time when we thought we knew what was best for us. We listened intently to the advice that Haruni gave us on what to wear that night and then into the next day. As long and as cold as it was on summit night, I can't imagine not heeding the advice of our guides.

As children, we often feel compelled to touch something that is hot, even after having been told by our parents not to. As a child we often seem to learn best the hard way. With age comes wisdom – enough wisdom to know that you should trust these guides who have climbed Kilimanjaro hundreds of times. We adopted the quote from Socrates, who said "I know that I am intelligent, because I know that I know nothing."

◌

Climbing Kilimanjaro for the first time really isn't that different than anything we do in life for the first time. Salespeople constantly encounter new experiences. Whether it be a new product, new industry or an objection you are hearing for the first time, learning takes longer when you do it on your own. You will gain wisdom through experience, but until you are able to gain your own wisdom, it helps to learn from those who have blazed the trail before you. The first thing to learn is you don't need to do it alone. Alone we can accomplish a lot, but through the wisdom and viewpoints of others, we can grow and learn more – and more quickly – in our sales careers. Likewise, if you follow and listen to the lessons from those who have already been successful, you will reach success much quicker than those who learn by trial and error alone. Remove the urge to say, "I can do it on my own." Humble yourself and focus on getting it right (not getting it right by yourself).

Two Ears, One Mouth

As salespeople, we tend to be gifted at speaking. But it might be that very gift that gets us into trouble. I was told early in my sales career that there was a reason God gave us two ears and one mouth: we should listen twice as much as we talk. In other words, listen first, talk second. The fact is, you rarely learn anything by talking. However, when you are listening, you are far more likely to gain useful information. As salespeople, however, we tend to act first and ask or listen second. While that might work sometimes, it can also cause a great deal of hardship. One of the best ways to be certain you are asking revealing questions is to write down 15 to 20 questions in advance of the meeting that are important to you and that you would like the prospect to answer. This will keep you focused on asking questions rather than talking too much. Listen to their answers carefully. You will be surprised how much more information the prospect will give you by using this powerful communication tool. You will almost always have an opportunity to talk after the prospect is done, but it doesn't always work that way in reverse. Talk first, and you run the risk of dissuading the prospect from sharing information with you that you could have learned. Why would a prospect bother answering some of your questions after they found out your product or service is outside of their budget? After all, they think they can't afford what you offer. The reality might be that after you understand the depths of their pain (and know that your offering can solve that pain), price is no longer an issue. Listen first, talk second.

The Wisdom of Following in the Footsteps of Success

There are people out there like Haruni and Ema for each of us. There are many people who have "hiked" the path you are on. Find a mentor who has walked in your shoes. Find someone who is more experienced than you or who is a more successful salesperson. Or talk to your sales manager. Find an expert to help you see down the road to anticipate or avoid unforeseen mistakes. A mentor can be a

129

source of inspiration – a person other than your sales manager. Someone who can motivate and push you to improve by giving you constructive criticism and advice for you to act on. Remember that you are also not held to having a single mentor. Seek out different mentors for different areas you wish to improve upon. You can seek a mentor for career growth, a mentor for advanced selling skills, and one for any area you seek to improve in your career. Since having a mentor is not a mandated action item, you will probably need to be the one who seeks out guidance and assistance in your career. But remember, not everyone will meet your specific needs, so be selective in your choice of mentors.

During our celebratory lunch at Bristol Cottages with Haruni and Ema, we learned that only 43% of those who attempt to summit Kilimanjaro successfully make it to the top. Two days? No, we were fortunate to be able to overcome Ema's prediction. The real story is that although we were in good shape and trained hard, we didn't make it to the top because of what we had read or thought we knew; we made it to the top because we followed the direction of those more experienced and who had gone before us. Will you do the same with your sales career? Seek out a mentor who has already navigated your route. Bottom line: having a mentor will get you to where you want to go faster, with fewer headaches.

CHAPTER 19

WHAT DO YOU KNOW FOR SURE?

As our Kilimanjaro adventure was coming to an end, it was difficult to say goodbye to Haruni and Ema. We had just finished lunch and it was time for them to go home to their families (Ema had a baby to hold!). We hoped we could come back to Tanzania sometime to see them again, but we weren't sure if that would actually happen. Seven days earlier we were complete strangers; yet when you spend most of every day with someone for that length of time, you no longer feel like strangers – you feel like lifelong friends. We told them that we have friends who are considering taking this trip and that we would certainly recommend them as our trusted guides. We told Ema, "If someone you meet for the first time already knows your name and they tell you that they are glad you are not dead, you'll know that Mama and Dadee sent them!" The reference to Ema's non-existent oximeter readings once again set us off into laughter – the kind of laughter that comes from inside jokes shared between long-time friends. We said goodbye and headed to our room for long overdue showers. I was surprised that Pam deferred and let me go first. I said, "Are you sure?" (but I said it only once), and then I quickly bolted into the bathroom and turned on

131

HOT water! I stepped in and began to laugh out loud at how good it felt to be clean again! It had been seven days since we had taken showers, and although pre-moistened towelettes help, they don't compare to the joy of a hot shower. I walked out of the bathroom beaming at how amazing I felt and Pam said she heard me laughing uncontrollably. She asked me if it really felt that good, and I replied, "You have no idea!" Ten minutes later I could hear her laughing from the shower, too. Ah, we felt human again!

Making the Call

It was now time to phone our family! We called our kids, Stefani and Kyle, first, and then our parents. It was difficult to relay all that had happened over the last week, but we did our best to give them the highlights. It was those very phone calls that had spurred me on through the most difficult parts of the climb. When it seemed too difficult to continue, I thought about how it would feel to call our family and tell them we didn't make it to the summit. I have no doubt that they would still have been proud of us, but I didn't want to make *that* call; I wanted to make *this* call – the phone call where we could be so proud to tell them that, while it was really difficult, we made it! During our calls, we told them all how much we loved them, and that we would soon be uploading pictures to Facebook to let the world know we had made it to the summit and conquered the fourth highest mountain in the world!

The rest of the afternoon and evening was spent looking at pictures and reliving the week we had just experienced. Very few of our conversations involved the mountain itself; we mostly spoke of our new friends. I went back to the journal I had used throughout the week and I looked at the page where I started a list about what I had learned on this trip. I had started this list on the second day of our trek and I continued to add to it as our journey continued. I want to share with you these ten things.

Ten Lessons from Kilimanjaro

1. The kindness and generosity of the Tanzanian people is overwhelming.

It is what Pam and I remember most about our trip. Tanzanians are humble and will do whatever is necessary, regardless of the impact on *them*. They serve you – not in the way a waiter serves a customer in a restaurant, but, rather, they serve your spirit and soul, not because they have to, but because they want to. They are very giving people. They don't just supply you with what you need, they are happy to do whatever they can for you. Iddi is the shining (or smiling) example. If he could bottle up his spirit and sell it, he would be rich beyond his dreams - and yet, he already is.

2. Age is not an issue.

Maybe this is something I want to believe more now than I did when I was in my 30's, but I wholeheartedly believe it to be true. I realize there will come a time when I can't do everything that someone half my age can do, but that time isn't right now! I am convinced more than ever, that if I train hard enough I can overcome what youth no longer provides. And if I can do it, you can do it! There is nothing special about me that makes it only possible for me to accomplish these things. I always knew that age brings you wisdom, but during our week on Kili I saw how wisdom can trump youth. I am a highly competitive person who loves to win, but sometimes slow and steady wins the race – sometimes the turtle really does beat the hare.

3. Pam and I can survive an entire week without showering.

Although it certainly won't be our regular practice to go a week without taking showers, we can do it. Pam also found out that she can go an entire week without putting on make-up – proving what I already knew to be the case – her beauty comes from within and doesn't need to be "made up." We also learned that we can be okay with dirt under our fingernails for a week. We fought it for the first couple of days, but when you are surrounded by nothing but rock and dirt, you quit fighting. I also found out that I can get a pretty good start on a beard in a week. *And I learned that part of letting go of who we were depended on embracing who we were becoming.* It was necessary to let go of the guy who wore slacks and dress shirts and who shaved and took a shower every day, to become the guy who could adapt to a dirt-covered, scree-littered mountain.

4. God has painted some amazing landscapes.

We appreciated the beauty in each of the five climate zones we travelled through. I saw places over the course of the week that I can't imagine can be chalked up to anything other than God's infinite wisdom and creativity, and I have found that to be true all over the world as well. We WALKED through clouds. I have flown in a plane many, many times and have looked down on clouds, but never have I looked down at them after having walked through them. At the summit, we were 10,000 feet above the clouds . . . I can't imagine that ever becoming ordinary. I found the scenery so compelling that I often stumbled on rocks because I was reveling in the view. Pam and I would joke about how we should keep our head down to avoid stumbling, but that was a small price to pay – we didn't want to miss what was next.

5. I am blessed.

Pam and I tell ourselves this often. I don't know why God has blessed us so much, but I am thankful. I know the definition of God's grace: getting what I don't deserve and could truly never earn. Pam and I have been very blessed to visit some amazing places. We are blessed to be healthy at our ages. We are blessed to be able to visit other countries and experience different cultures. We are blessed to live a life that I didn't even dream of 30 years ago.

6. People really aren't that different.

We might be 8,000 miles apart and culturally diverse, but when it comes down to it, we really aren't that different. We all love to laugh and get the most out of life. We love our families and can't wait to get home to see them. We have successes. We have struggles. We long to make personal connections with one another. We might look different, but we aren't really different at all.

7. *We needed everything we brought on our trip.*

The countless trips to REI were worth it. We needed the water purification pills so our "western stomachs" would not suffer. On summit night, we needed all the clothing we brought — anything less and we would have frozen. We needed the trekking poles. I can't imagine how loud my knees would have screamed if I wouldn't have been able to transfer some of my weight onto them. We needed the granola bars as snacks between meals to keep up our energy. We needed the utility knife to tighten Pam's trekking pole when it kept collapsing. All our research and preparation was worth it. We needed everything we brought.

8. *Porters on Kilimanjaro are amazing!*

They are first up in the morning and the last to bed. Many porters wear tire treads with rope for shoes, yet they walked by me as if I were standing still. They make less than half of 1% of what I make and they work harder and are more giving than I am. They worked seven days straight, washed their upper bodies in a trough shared by others, had a few hours break, then set off for another seven-day trip. If the porters I saw had access to the resources we have in the United States, they would rule the world. Words can't adequately explain the work ethic, quality of work and kindness that these amazing people exhibit.

9. *We can live without access to all forms of electronic communication (for a while, at least).*

Our phones didn't work most of the time so we just turned them off... and we survived. And get this: when Pam and I were alone in our tent, we talked to one another! (Scary, huh?) As funny as it was for us to do without our reliance on electronic devices for a week, we noticed that almost everyone in Tanzania has a cell phone. I think they use their phones more often that we do. We even saw a woman carrying a large container of water on her head while talking on a phone! But we enjoyed being able to "unplug" for a while. We just focused on communicating with each other face-to-face. What a concept, right?

10. My wife is tougher than I ever imagined.

We have been married for 28 years and I have known her for 33 years. When 33 of your 51 years are with the same person, you tend to think there are no more secrets. There were very few women on Kilimanjaro that week, and far fewer Pam's age. My guess would be you could count the amount of women her age on the mountain that week on one hand. The trek was very physically demanding and she kept going when many men stopped. She kept going near the summit when she felt really bad. I believe she found a level of determination that not even she knew she had. I am proud to tell you that I didn't know that about my wife.

Resonance

I have many memories from our trip, but those ten items continue to resonate for me. There were moments in our trip where there was uncertainty. I don't know if I could have made it through the first day without Haruni's help. I don't know what my viewpoint would have been about the Kilimanjaro Kids Care Orphanage if we had simply dropped off the supplies instead of making a personal visit. What I *do* know are the ten lessons I shared with you. I *know* how amazing porters are, I *know* how tough my wife is, I *know* how blessed I am. And isn't it great to know something for certain, to know it so deeply in your soul, rather than to just wonder?

☙

I have conducted weekly one-on-one sales meetings with sales representatives for more than 25 years, and I often hear the phrases "I think," "I believe," "My gut tells me," and "I'm pretty sure" when I ask them about an opportunity they are working on. I follow up by asking them what they know for sure. Their response is always less assured. They often aren't certain that they know *anything* for sure. I ask them how they can remove that uncertainty and find out what they want to know for sure. Their answer? "I guess I can ask them." Ding, ding! There is your answer. It is so easy, yet so difficult. Asking questions reveals the truth behind the opportunity, objection, etc.

When You Make Assumptions...

I didn't know if I could handle the altitude above 19,000 feet and I wasn't sure if I could handle 17 hours of hiking in one day. The only way I could know for sure was to test myself and find out. We need to be careful not to assume what we think we know. In sales, the most important thing you can do to help people buy a real solution is to understand them and what they want. When we assume things about someone, we stop ourselves from learning more about them. Let's face it. We all have to make assumptions about our customers. There is a myth in selling that assumptions are bad. Assumptions aren't bad in themselves. It's our unconscious reliance on them that causes problems. There is no way we can possibly know everything about our customers. We *must* make certain assumptions. But one of the traits of a great salesperson is someone who can distinguish the difference between facts and assumptions. Knowing the difference between fact and assumption is critical to success in selling. Test your assumptions by asking questions to overcome ambiguity. Ask yourself, "How do I know this?" "How have I verified this?" Assume everything you know is, well, an assumption. It's the unrecognized assumptions that harm us – not the ones we know.

Asking Questions to Overcome Objections

As I mentioned, the best method to discover the truth is to ask questions...quickly. Anyone who has ever watched an episode of the police show Dragnet has heard Sergeant Joe Friday's memorable words, "All we want are the facts, ma'am." The show illustrated the importance of uncovering the truth and uncovering it quickly. In addition to adding suspense to the show, the facts that Sergeant Friday collected were often concealed, a reality we face in the selling world. Asking the right questions provided the foundation for his detective and forensic work. Similarly, a set of questions to quickly uncover everything you need to know throughout the sales cycle will help increase your percentage of successful outcomes. As with Dragnet, salespeople know that the right answers are the result of asking the right questions. They also know that the processes to rapidly find, collect, analyze, and interpret the truth make the difference between success and failure. The questions we asked Haruni on the night before we reached the summit were important, because the consequences of our assumptions could have been dangerous. Making an incorrect assumption and not wearing enough clothing while being exposed to a wind chill of -27 degrees Fahrenheit for eight hours could have had far-reaching implications. Losing a sale isn't life or death, but there isn't any reason to not ask the right questions to avoid whatever consequences you will face.

Great salespeople know that customers will tell them most everything they need to know, if given the right opportunity. Our job is to put our customers in a position to do so. When reviewing a salesperson's or company's sales pipeline, I find that many opportunities have appeared to "stall out." The once eager prospect has now gone "radio silent." I am told that the prospect was very interested and now they won't return your phone call. In this situation, there is typically *something you don't know* that is working against you. Among the possibilities:

- The person you were talking to can't make the final decision and you weren't talking to the ultimate decision maker.
- You assumed your solution completely solved their needs and it doesn't.
- They don't have enough money in their budget and will have to wait until next year.

- Your solution is lower on their priority list than you assumed.

The list of possible reasons goes on and on. But you could probably resolve issues like these with a question. For example, asking, "Who, in addition to yourself, will be involved with making the final decision?" would have avoided the problem of identifying whether there was another decision maker without offending the person you were talking to. Each of these issues *became* an issue because an assumption wasn't validated by asking a question. You will be surprised what your customers will tell you if you ask them a question.

Sales is a lot like our trip to the summit in that it can be difficult enough to move forward without adding incorrect assumptions to the equation. Some of our assumptions don't have significant consequences, but some do. Not having the proper clothing for summit night could have been disastrous. Not knowing that the solution you suggested to a prospect doesn't "remove their pain" — when you have another solution that does — is also disastrous. Dressing properly for summit night and offering your prospect the proper solution comes from asking the right questions. The truth is there for you to uncover. All you have to do is ask!

CHAPTER 20

SHARE YOUR KNOWLEDGE

S ince coming home to Indiana, we've had some difficulty explaining this trip when asked about our experience. No other trip we've made has included such an immersion into a culture. We find ourselves responding by saying, "It was great," and, "We had a lot of fun," and "Yes, we made it to the top." Yet those phrases seem far too inadequate. How do you explain in a few short sentences that this trip forever caused a change in us so profound that we will never be the same people again?

Luckily, we have had opportunities to share more than just a few sentences. We have been invited into our friends' homes to share our pictures and our stories. Of course, there are hundreds of photographs – including when we arrived at the summit and at various places along our trek – but more often than not, we talk about the Tanzanian people. And more specifically, about their *kindness*. This is what we remember most and what has stayed in our hearts. Don't get me wrong, we certainly remember our achievement – getting to the summit – but that's not what we reflect on the most. Rather, there are four stories in particular that we share every time we talk about our adventure:

The Hugs of a Resilient Child

We'll never forget the hugs Peter gave us at the Kilimanjaro Kids Care Orphanage. We share with others how Peter squeezed a little harder and hugged us a little longer than the other children. How he threw the soccer ball back and forth with Pam for an hour and how he just stood next to her after they were done playing. We smile when we think about how he just wanted to be near her. We think about his terrible past and how he has been able to overcome tremendous misery and pain to become that young boy who is always smiling. We remember all the children, of course, but Peter's name and face come to mind first when we think about that amazing day.

Surviving the First Day

We remember how I almost didn't make it through Day One because of food poisoning. I think about how Haruni showed great patience as I had to stop often and sit down. How he wouldn't take "no" for an answer when I told him I could still carry all the items in my backpack. I think about how much I appreciated the caring and concern he extended, when it was only the first day and we didn't really know one another. The kind of caring that Haruni exhibited comes from the heart, not out of sense of obligation.

A Giving Spirit

I often tell of Iddi bringing us fruit juice and a snack when we were getting dehydrated as we came down from the summit. That story often makes me emotional when I tell it and many have shed tears as I shared this story of the grace he offered. I think about how happy he was to help us. He barely spoke any English, yet he understood how badly we needed help and I remember how pleased he was that he could be there for us. I remember how that three-hour round trip to bring us food and drink wasn't enough; he insisted on carrying our backpack the rest of the way to Barafu Camp. Iddi exhibited that same giving spirit the entire week in everything he did. It is, simply, who he is.

America

This last story I have not shared with you yet. Following our trek up Kilimanjaro we went on safari and had a single guide the entire week; his name was Stuart. He was 24 years old and had taken classes at the local university for a few years, learning every aspect of how to be a Safari guide, in addition to honing his English. We spent all day with Stuart in the same way we spent time with Haruni and Ema. Stuart was a bit more reserved, but by the fourth day he started to open up to us and we got to know each other better. At one point during the week, I asked Stuart what his impression of America was. He looked at me with surprise and repeated my question: "What do I think about America?" he asked. "Yes," I said, and then I proceeded to tell him that it didn't matter what he answered – that there was no right answer, good or bad. I wondered what he even knew about America, given that most of the television stations were from Africa or India. He had already shared with me that only the "richest of the rich" in Tanzania were able to afford computers, so I assumed whatever he knew about America might be limited. I also thought his knowledge about America might come from politics or Hollywood, news that might be more widely distributed. I was ready to tell him how politicians and people from Hollywood don't really represent what and who America is. But his answer to my question caught Pam and me totally off guard. What Stuart said was this: "*I think America is heaven.*"

His response was not what I expected and for once I was speechless for a while; but I finally responded and asked, "Why do you say that?" Stuart answered by asking, "If I go to America, can't I become whoever I want to be?" I told him he could, but that America wasn't perfect and we had our share of problems. Still, I knew what he said about our country was true, and hearing the words he chose – and how he said them – made me think once again about how blessed we are.

Stuart asked me how many people are out of work in America. I told him the last few years had been more difficult and the unemployment rate was "about 8%." Stuart responded by saying, "Eight percent work?" I told him, "No, 8% of Americans do *not* have jobs." He nodded that he understood. I then asked him what the unemployment rate was in Tanzania. His answer shocked me: 97%. We had just spent the last week and a half with those fortunate few in "the 3%" of employed Tanzanians.

Keeping the Story Alive

Pam and I feel it is important that the lessons we learned do not stop with us. We spoke in front of our church about the orphanage and how their contributions made such an incredible difference. I have talked with many friends, acquaintances and even clients about the amazing spirit of the African people. This very book is an effort to share some insights into how our trip impacted us and, by extension, perhaps it will impact *you*.

It is good to share your experiences and your wisdom with others. We found one exception to that rule, however. On the morning following our return from Kilimanjaro, we were once again eating breakfast at Bristol Cottages as we had done exactly one week before. But now we were the couple transitioning from our Kilimanjaro trek to a safari. We were waiting on Stuart's arrival, with our hiking duffel bags and our suitcases arranged just outside the café, when six "twenty-somethings" at the next table looked at our gear and said, "Did you just get back from hiking up Kilimanjaro?" We said, "Yes." They then asked us how hard it was. I looked at Pam, smiled slightly, and answered, "The summit night was tough."

CR

Sharing information with your prospects and your clients is an integral part of selling, but don't forget that the intent of your messaging, however, is very important. Do you like selling? I love gaining new clients, but I'm not a fan of selling. I prefer to be a "non-salesperson." I like finding a prospect that will benefit from use of my product or service. I want to be the conduit to help the customer select products or services that will solve their needs. The reason that some people have a negative view of salespeople is because they believe we don't have their best interests at heart – and unfortunately some don't. Haruni had my best interest at heart when he allowed me to take time to recover on Day One. He wasn't concerned with keeping a schedule or dinner being served late; his only concern was for me. If all salespeople followed that model, prospective customers would probably take every meeting! As salespeople, we need to be non-manipulative – we need to close a sale by always being truthful. We need to be helpful, not pushy. We need to be consultative by making meaningful recommendations and walking away when our solution isn't the best for our prospect. We need to have complete product knowledge, so we can have the knowledge needed to help a customer make an informed decision or solve a problem. Imagine if our whole goal was to serve the customer – how different would our customers feel? Probably the way I feel about Haruni.

Knowledge Fluency

Organizations need to make sure that their sales teams are experts in knowing and representing their products and services. Indeed, best-in-class sales organizations are markedly better in overall product and service knowledge. They understand how to use that knowledge to understand their prospect's business challenges and map solutions to address them. Organizations can facilitate this methodology by embracing the concept of sales knowledge fluency. If your people cannot speak fluently about your product and service offerings, and ask the right questions to uncover specific needs that your solutions fulfill, then they are not optimizing their performance. You get to fluency by providing your team with the proper tools and then testing their competency. Testing isn't about finding out what they don't know; it is about finding out their competency level and providing them with the information and training needed to fill that gap. Customers are more likely to trust salespeople who show confidence in themselves and what they are selling. You can build this confidence by increasing your knowledge of your organization's products or services.

Sharing your knowledge with a prospect also builds trust. I am not suggesting that you get into "tell mode," I am suggesting that you share the type of information with a prospect that they are seeking and that will benefit them. Because it is universally accepted that before anyone will buy from you they need to know, like, and trust you, there is no better way to help people in this process than to openly share your knowledge. By sharing needed knowledge with your prospect, you break down the barriers between you and your prospect and position yourself as an expert. You end up attracting the people who want to benefit from your expertise. This attraction is important because it helps you build your sales pipeline by attracting your perfect customers. By sharing your knowledge, and seeing how this knowledge is helping people, you also pass on your passion for your product and services.

My Hope for You

Sales is a wonderful profession. It provides you with freedom, tremendous earning potential, flexibility in schedule and the ability to meet many new people. That might be why Haruni and Ema enjoy what they do so much. They have a chance to work outdoors, be paid on performance, not be held to a daily work schedule, and meet new people every week. My hope for you is that you adopt the principles that Haruni and Ema embrace. If you do, your customers will become raving fans and you will be among the very best in your profession.

As a servant leader who just happens to be a top sales professional, you might find yourself feeling as blessed as I do. And one day, as you look back over a life of abundance and success, you'll

145

see that you have indeed lived beyond the mountaintop!

SPECIAL THANKS TO OUR AMAZING TEAM FROM KINDOROKO TOURS

Haruni Mshahara (Chief Guide)

Emmanuel "Ema" William (Assistant Guide)

Minihaji Mshahara (Cook)

Iddi Juma (Waiter)

Abubakari "Giligilani" Lohai

Hamisi Juma

Isa Omari

Rajabu Zuberi

Hokelai Stivini

Hatibu Mishughuli

Salimu Bakari

Ombeni Rashidi

Adamu Isa

Gloria Moshi, Owner, Kindoroko Tours

ABOUT THE AUTHOR

Mark Thacker is the Founder and Owner of Propelis Consulting, a company specializing in the implementation of sales strategy, sales process and sales execution for businesses of varied size. Mark is also the co-owner of Sales Xceleration, an organization that provides successful Vice Presidents of Sales with the necessary tools to establish their own consulting business. Mark has a 30-year history of sales leadership and success in diverse industries. A natural leader and motivator, Mark has led sales teams with annual revenue responsibility from $1 million to in excess of $800 million.

Mark earned his Bachelor's and Master's Degrees from Butler University, where he is a long-standing basketball season ticket holder and ardent supporter. In addition to travelling and climbing tall mountains, Mark enjoys running and golfing. An Elder in his church, Mark also participates on the Missions Team and leads an annual outreach event called the Day of Caring. His goal is to live out faith, family and friends -- in that order.

Mark and his wife, Pam, reside in Fishers, Indiana, a suburb of Indianapolis. They have been married since 1986 and have two adult children, Stefani and Kyle. They provide him with his favorite title in life . . . Dad.